Incredibly Easy
Light
Cooking

Publications International, Ltd.

Favorite Brand Name Recipes at www.fbnr.com

Nutritional Analysis: Linda R. Yoakam, M.S., R.D., L.D.

Pictured on the front cover: Enlightened Pineapple Upside-Down Cake *(page 138).*
Pictured on the back cover: Winter Squash Soup *(page 44).*

ISBN-13: 978-1-4127-2552-1
ISBN-10: 1-4127-2552-6

Library of Congress Control Number: 2006931333

Manufactured in China.

8 7 6 5 4 3 2 1

Nutritional Analysis: Every effort has been made to check the accuracy of the nutritional information that appears with each recipe. However, because numerous variables account for a wi range of values for certain foods, nutritive analyses in this book should be considered approximate Different results may be obtained by using different nutrient databases and different brand-name products.

Microwave Cooking: Microwave ovens vary in wattage. Use the cooking times as guidelines and check for doneness before adding more time.

Preparation/Cooking Times: Preparation times are based on the approximate amount of time required to assemble the recipe before cooking, baking, chilling or serving. These times include preparation steps such as measuring, chopping and mixing. The fact that some preparations and cooking can be done simultaneously is taken into account. Preparation of optional ingredients and serving suggestions is not included.

Note: This book is for informational purposes and is not intended to provide medical advice. Neither Publications International, Ltd., nor the authors, editors or publisher takes responsibility fc any possible consequences from any treatment, procedure, exercise, dietary modification, action, c applications of medication or preparation by any person reading or following the information in th cookbook. The publication of this book does not constitute the practice of medicine, and this cookbook does not attempt to replace your physician, pharmacist or health-care specialist. **Before undertaking any course of treatment or nutrition plan, the authors, editors and publisher advise the reader to check with a physician or other health-care provider.**

Contents

Healthy Eating for Life

It's simple: To lose weight, you have to use more calories than you consume. The good news is that there are many easy ways to start eating better. Combine this with regular exercise, and you're on your way to losing weight. If you don't need to lose weight, **Incredibly Easy Light Cooking** will help you to enjoy more healthful foods and get you on the road to healthy eating—for the rest of your life.

The Fat Connection

Since fat is made up of nearly two times as many calories as either protein or carbohydrate, cutting fat is the quickest and easiest way to cut calories. Plus, by limiting the amount of fat you eat, you won't be only cutting calories. You'll also reduce your chances for heart disease, cancer and even diabetes. Saturated fats, found in animal products and coconut oil, palm kernel oil and palm oil; hydrogenated fats found in processed foods such as crackers and cookies; and cholesterol are notorious for contributing to health problems. If you eat less fat, you'll also be consuming less of these unhealthy types of fat.

Making a change to low-fat living doesn't have to mean major sacrifices. You can still eat foods that taste good without spending a lot of time in the kitchen. The key word is "substitute." Find low-fat, reduced-fat and fat-free alternatives for the foods you love, and you'll be more apt to stick to your new low-fat eating plan. And find new ways to prepare and season foods without fat. This cookbook offers you a wonderful selection of low-fat recipes.

Tips for Reducing Fat in Your Diet

- Always have fresh fruits and vegetables on hand. Take some to work with you, too. They're great fat-free alternatives to the high-fat, nutrient-deprived foods in vending machines.

- Get rid of high-fat foods and snacks in your house. You won't indulge if the temptation is not there. Instead, snack on fat-free, high-fiber fruits, vegetables and whole-grain crackers.

- Use fat-free and low-fat products in place of their high-fat counterparts. Fat-free and low-fat salad dressings, mayonnaise, sour cream, cheeses and yogurt are just a few examples of products on the market today. Most of the items can be used without greatly affecting the flavors of the finished dishes. Or try mixing the fat-free product with the low-fat product.

- If you typically drink whole milk, try 2% for awhile. You'll notice a difference at first, but it won't be long until you will likely prefer the reduced-fat 2% milk over the whole milk. Next, try 1% milk, and finally fat-free (skim). Many people who swear they'll drink nothing other than whole milk, with time, often find they tend to prefer skim milk.

Spread jams and jellies, rather than butter and margarine, on breads.

Prepare more mixed meat and vegetable dishes. Cut the amount of meat in the recipe by one third and increase the amount of vegetables by one third.

Cook with oil instead of butter. Use canola for a neutral flavor or olive oil. If you really feel you need the taste of butter for a favorite dish, replace half of it with oil.

Change your salad dressing. Instead of store-bought salad dressings loaded with sugar or preservatives, make a simple homemade vinaigrette with olive oil, balsamic vinaigrette and herbs.

Cook at home. Deep-fried chicken, potatoes and fish from restaurants are very likely to contain high levels of bad trans fats. Home-cooked meals are almost always healthier than fast food.

Eat more fish. Fatty fish, such as salmon and tuna, contain beneficial omega-3 fatty acids. These fats appear to improve cholesterol, so opt for fish instead of meat once or twice a week. Fish like cod, flounder, halibut, perch and red snapper are low in fat and a perfect choice for eating light. Choose baking, broiling or grilling rather than frying for all fish.

Spend More Time in the Produce Aisle

One of the best things you can do for your health is to eat more vegetables and fruit. Between 5 and 10 (½-cup) servings are recommended daily. Of course, attention must be paid to the kind of vegetables and how they are prepared. Super-sizing your order of French fries will not improve your diet! Experts agree that the best idea is to choose a wide variety of produce from a rainbow of different colors.

Choosing by color is fun, but there is a serious reason behind it. In addition to vitamins and minerals, fruits and vegetables are packed with powerful natural plant compounds—nutritionists call these phytochemicals or phytonutrients. The same compounds that give produce its color may keep us healthier because they contain antioxidants. (An antioxidant is a compound that can protect our bodies from damaging molecules that are created naturally in our bodies that cause aging or disease.) Different colors of produce offer different combinations of these health-giving compounds, so it's important to eat a variety of colors. These nutrients don't come in a vitamin pill either.

It is also best to avoid peeling fruits and vegetables if you can, since the peel often contains the most nutrients. Beware of adding a lot of fatty dressings or sauces which can add calories. Brighten the clean, refreshing flavors of vegetables and fruit with a few drops of fresh lemon juice or just enjoy them plain.

Tips for Adding Vegetables and Fruits to Your Diet

- Buy pre-washed bags of vegetables or bring home goodies from the salad bar at your local supermarket.

- Instead of grabbing cookies or a soda, keep baby carrots, celery sticks, cherry tomatoes or sugar snap peas on hand for snacking.

- Once a week, plan a whole meal around a vegetable-based main dish. Try a stir-fry, soup or pasta creation.

- Add veggies to your favorite foods. If you have to have pizza, order it with vegetable toppings. Shred carrots or zucchini into meat loaf or muffins. Grill portobellos, bell peppers and zucchini along with your burgers or hot dogs.

- Try something new and different. Add color and new flavors to your menus with less common vegetables like Asian eggplant, kale or parsnips. Or, different varieties of common vegetables like Italian-style green beans.

- Grow vegetables in your own garden or visit a nearby farmer's market or produce stand. In-season fresh vegetables are so delicious they make it easy to get your vitamins.

- Pair vegetables with fiber-rich legumes and whole grains. Fiber gives the feeling of fullness without extra fat.

Who Needs Fiber?

We all do, and most of us don't get enough. Current recommendations suggest 20 to 35 grams of dietary fiber per day, yet the average American eats only 14 to 15 grams. Studies about whether fiber can help reduce the risk of diseases such as diabetes and heart disease are inconclusive and still underway, but there is no doubt that fiber is an important part of a healthy diet.

Fiber is the indigestible part of a carbohydrate. Foods high in fiber slow down the absorption of glucose and help keep you feeling full longer. One kind of fiber even helps reduce levels of bad cholesterol (LDL) in your bloodstream.

Tips to Add More Fiber to Your Diet

Try oatmeal or another whole-grain cereal for breakfast.

Switch to whole-grain bread. Make sure the label says whole-grain or whole wheat, not "made with whole wheat."

Snack on sweet whole fruit instead of candy or cookies.

Add more beans or lentils to your diet.

Snack on crunchy raw veggies instead of chips or crackers.

Eating Away from Home

Try to eat out less, and eat less fast food. Take a healthy packed lunch to work. If you don't have time to prepare it in the morning, pack and refrigerate it the night before.

Snack at home before going out to eat. You'll have more control when you're ordering.

Ask your server how a dish is prepared, and ask for low-fat menu suggestions.

Opt for yeast-type breads and rolls, which tend to be lower in fat than muffins, corn bread and biscuits. Choose whole-grain breads that are higher in fiber. They will make you feel fuller.

Ask for salad dressings and sauces to be served on the side. Dip your fork into the salad dressing before picking up a bite of salad.

"Loin" and "round" signal leaner cuts of beef, while "loin" and "leg" refer to leaner cuts of pork, lamb and veal.

Preparing Foods

Buy lean cuts of meat and trim off any visible fat before cooking. Remove the skin from poultry or buy skinless pieces from your grocer.

Purchase extra-lean ground beef, pork and turkey. Rinse the liquid fat off the meat after it is cooked and before adding the other ingredients.

Use extra-lean ground round or turkey for meat loaf, meatballs and other recipes that make it difficult to drain excess fat.

Choose boneless skinless chicken breasts instead of drumsticks, thighs and wings.

- Use a fat separator or baster to remove the fat from soups, stews, sauces and casseroles. Or chill these dishes in the refrigerator overnight, then skim the congealed fat from the top of the food the next day.

- Make low-fat, high-fiber grain and vegetable dishes the main focus of your meal and make meat a condiment, just to add a bit of flavor.

- Roast lean meats and poultry on a rack to allow any extra fat to drip off.

- Drain the fat from meats cooked in a skillet.

- Eat water-packed tuna instead of oil-packed tuna.

- Bake, steam, roast, broil, grill, microwave, poach or boil foods instead of frying.

- Buy the heaviest (best) nonstick cookware you can afford. You won't have to use any or as much fat for sautéing.

- Use flavored nonstick cooking sprays to keep foods from sticking to skillets and pans instead of oil or butter.

- Use only half the fat called for in your favorite recipes. If you are using the fat for sautéing, be sure to reduce the heat to medium-high and stir the food often.

- Measure any oil called for in a recipe. Don't just "eyeball" it.

- Sauté vegetables in flavored liquids such as wine, broth, bouillon, tomato juice or sherry instead of butter and oil. Just be sure to use as little water as possible to cook foods because water dilutes flavors.

- Replace some or all of the oil in baked goods with applesauce, mashed banana, puréed fruit or plain fat-free yogurt. Use trial and error to come up with the correct proportions. Start by substituting half the fat with the fat-free replacement. Since low-fat baked goods tend to dry out easier than their full-fat counterparts, be sure to keep a close eye on them during the last five minutes of baking.

- Substitute 2 egg whites or ¼ cup egg substitute for 1 egg.

- Use cornstarch or flour mixed with water, rice, potatoes or other puréed vegetables in place of cream and butter to thicken sauces and soups.

- Add spice to your fat-free and low-fat meals. Spices compensate for the lack of fat, adding loads of incomparable flavor. Use spices, herbs, marinades, flavored vinegars, fat-free salad dressings, cocktail sauce, lemon juice and salsa to flavor foods, instead of high-fat sauces and salad dressings, sour cream, butter and oils. Bring out the flavor in dry spices by sautéing them in a pan over medium heat before adding them to foods.

What About Dessert?

This book includes a chapter of delicious dessert recipes. Eating well for the rest of your life should be enjoyable. Don't deprive yourself of dessert, but choose a luscious fruit-based dessert or a low-fat low-calorie treat, like those in this book. If you do need to give in occasionally to something decadent, eat a small portion and enjoy it.

Keep Moving!

You don't have to run a marathon to benefit from daily physical activity. The benefits go way beyond just helping you control your weight. Exercising will boost your metabolism, relieve stress and help you sleep better. If you're intimidated by the time and expense of joining the gym, anything you can do to add motion to your life will help. Once you start, you may be surprised at how much better you feel.

Tips for Getting Active Without Joining a Gym

Get a pedometer and use it to stay fit by walking about 10,000 steps every day (that's about five miles).

Turn off the TV. Take the kids out to play with the dog or toss a baseball instead.

Take the stairs. Think of a flight of stairs as an opportunity to burn a few calories. Avoid elevators and escalators.

Make reading a physical activity. Ride a stationary bike, walk on a treadmill or do leg lifts as you read the mail or the morning paper.

Add some exercise to your chores. Walk the dog at a faster pace. Do lunges while you vacuum or turn on peppy music and dance through the dusting.

How to Use the Recipes in this Book.

Every recipe has nutritional information, including the number of calories and grams of fat. These numbers are approximate and intended to be guidelines only. Garnishes, serving suggestions and optional ingredients are NOT included in the calculations. Where a range of amounts or a choice of ingredients is shown in the ingredients list, the first item listed was used for nutritional calculations. Since the numbers are based on individual servings, it's important to take portion size into consideration to get an accurate nutritional picture. Most recipes have 10 grams of fat or less per serving and provide 30% or less of total calories from fat.

Feta-Stuffed Tomato (p. 12)

Mediterranean Bread B
(p. 28)

Marinated Artichoke
Cheese Toasts (p. 24)

Warm Pullaparts (p. 20)

Tasty Appetizers

Feta-Stuffed Tomatoes

Prep Time: 5 minutes

2 small plum tomatoes (about ¼ pound)
⅓ cup chopped seeded cucumber
1 tablespoon chopped fresh mint
1 tablespoon crumbled reduced-fat feta cheese
1 tablespoon fat-free sour cream
½ teaspoon finely grated lemon peel
¼ teaspoon black pepper

1. Cut tomatoes lengthwise into halves. Scoop out and discard pulp, leaving ¼-inch-thick shells. Place tomato shells, cut sides down, on paper towels to drain.

2. Combine cucumber, mint, feta cheese, sour cream, lemon peel and pepper in small bowl. Spoon mixture into tomato shells.

Makes 4 serving

Nutrients per Serving (1 stuffed tomato half): Calories: 16, Total Fat: <1 g, Calories from Fat: 18%, Saturated Fat: <1 g, Cholesterol: 1 mg, Sodium: 31 mg, Carbohydrate: 2 g, Dietary Fiber: 1 g, Protein: 1 g

Dietary Exchanges: Free

Bean Spread Cracker Stackers

1 can (15 ounces) kidney beans, rinsed and drained
1 tablespoon *each* **sour cream and cider vinegar**
2 teaspoons dried parsley
2 cloves crushed garlic
½ teaspoon *each* **salt and ground cumin**
½ teaspoon hot pepper sauce
90 baked whole-wheat snack crackers

1. Place beans, sour cream, vinegar, parsley, garlic, salt, cumin and hot sauce in food processor or blender; process until smooth. Transfer bean mixture to bowl; cover and refrigerate at least 1 hour to allow flavors to blend.

2. To make stackers, spread 1 teaspoon bean dip on 1 cracker. Top with second cracker. Spread 1 teaspoon bean dip on second cracker. Top with third cracker. Repeat with remaining bean mixture and crackers. Serve immediately.   *Makes 30 serving*

Tip: If you don't want to make all of the stackers at once, refrigerate the bean spread. It will keep for up to one week. You can also use the bean spread as a dip with baked tortilla chips.

Nutrients per Serving (1 stacker): Calories: 67, Total Fat: 2 g, Calories from Fat: 27%, Saturated Fat: 1 g, Cholesterol: 0 mg, Sodium: 135 mg, Carbohydrate: 11 g, Dietary Fiber: 2 g, Protein: 2 g

Dietary Exchanges: 1 Starch

Tasty "Fun"due

1 cup cheese sauce
2 cups *each* broccoli florets and snow peas
4 ounces cooked chicken breast*
4 ounces cooked beef cut into 1-inch chunks**
4 ounces French bread cut into 1-inch cubes, warmed if
    desired
1 cup grape or cherry tomatoes

Try using frozen cooked chicken breast chunks or strips.

Try using frozen cooked beef chunks or strips.

. Place cheese sauce in small microwavable bowl. Cover and heat about minute. To keep cheese sauce warm, pour into fondue pot or small slow ooker on LOW heat.

. Meanwhile, bring 2 cups water to a boil in large saucepan over high eat. Add broccoli and snow peas. Cover and remove from heat. Let stand minutes. Drain and set aside.

. Warm chicken and beef chunks on medium microwavable plate on IGH 2 minutes.

. Arrange broccoli, snow peas, chicken, beef, bread cubes and tomatoes n serving tray. Serve with cheese sauce.   *Makes 4 servings*

utrients per Serving (¼ of total recipe): Calories: 262, Total Fat: 8 g, alories from Fat: 27%, Saturated Fat: 3 g, Cholesterol: 74 mg, Sodium: 655 mg, arbohydrate: 23 g, Dietary Fiber: 3 g, Protein: 25 g

ietary Exchanges: 1 Starch, 1 Vegetable, 3 Lean Meat

Hot or Cold Tuna Snacks

4 ounces reduced-fat cream cheese
1 can (6 ounces) water-packed chunk light tuna, well draine
1 tablespoon *each* **minced onion and chopped fresh parsley**
½ teaspoon *each* **dried oregano and black pepper**
18 (½-inch-thick) slices seedless cucumber
18 capers* (optional)

*Capers are the flower buds of a bush native to the Mediterranean and parts of India. The buds are picked, sun-dried, then pickled. Capers should be rinsed before using to remove excess salt.

1. Combine cream cheese, tuna, onion, parsley, oregano and pepper in medium bowl; mix well.

2. Mound about 1 tablespoon tuna mixture to completely cover top of each cucumber slice. To serve cold, place on serving plate and garnish with capers.

3. To serve hot, preheat oven to 500°F. Spray baking sheet with nonstick cooking spray. Place snacks on prepared baking sheet and bake about 10 minutes or until tops are puffed and brown. Transfer to serving plate and garnish with capers. *Makes 6 serving*

Nutrients per Serving (3 snacks): Calories: 83, Total Fat: 5 g, Calories from Fat: 44%, Saturated Fat: 2 g, Cholesterol: 21 mg, Sodium: 196 mg, Carbohydrate: 2 g, Dietary Fiber: <1 g, Protein: 9 g

Dietary Exchanges: 1 Lean Meat, ½ Fat

Corn Tortilla Chips

12 corn tortillas (6-inch diameter), preferably day-old*
Vegetable oil
½ to 1 teaspoon salt

If tortillas are fresh, let stand, uncovered, in single layer on wire rack 1 to 2 hours to dry slightly.

1. Stack 6 tortillas; cutting through stack, cut into 6 equal wedges. Repea with remaining tortillas.

2. Heat ½ inch oil in deep, heavy, large skillet over medium-high heat to 375°F; adjust heat to maintain temperature.

3. Fry tortilla wedges in single layer 1 minute or until crisp, turning occasionally. Remove with slotted spoon; drain on paper towels. Repeat until all chips have been fried. Sprinkle chips with salt.

Makes 6 dozen chip

Tip: Tortilla chips are served with salsa, used as the base for nachos and used as scoops for guacamole, refried beans or other dips. They are best eaten fresh, but can be stored, tightly covered, in cool place 2 or 3 days. Reheat in 350°F oven a few minutes before serving.

Nutrients per Serving (6 chips): Calories: 57, Total Fat: 1 g, Calories from Fat: 10%, Saturated Fat: <1 g, Cholesterol: 0 mg, Sodium: 40 mg, Carbohydrate: 12 g, Dietary Fiber: 0 g, Protein: 1 g
Dietary Exchanges: 1 Starch

Pepperoni Pizza Dip

1 package (8 ounces) fat-free cream cheese
½ cup fat-free sour cream
1 teaspoon dried oregano
⅛ teaspoon *each* **garlic powder and ground red pepper**
½ cup tomato pizza sauce
½ cup chopped turkey pepperoni
½ cup chopped red onion
½ cup chopped green bell pepper
½ cup (2 ounces) shredded low-fat mozzarella cheese
Red bell pepper strips, broccoli florets and/or pita chips (optional)

1. Preheat oven to 350°F. Beat cream cheese, sour cream, oregano, garlic powder and ground red pepper in large bowl with electric mixer on low speed until smooth. Spread in 9-inch pie pan. Spread pizza sauce over top.

2. Sprinkle with pepperoni, onion and green bell pepper. Bake 10 minutes. Remove from oven; top with cheese. Bake 5 minutes more or until cheese is melted and dip is heated through.

3. Serve with red bell pepper strips, broccoli and toasted pita chips, if desired. *Makes 12 servings*

Nutrients per Serving (2 tablespoons dip without dippers): Calories: 76, Total Fat: 4 g, Calories from Fat: 47%, Saturated Fat: 2 g, Cholesterol: 20 mg, Sodium: 244 mg, Carbohydrate: 4 g, Dietary Fiber: <1 g, Protein: 5 g

Dietary Exchanges: 1 Lean Meat, 1 Fat

Warm Pullaparts

Prep Time: 5 minutes • **Bake Time:** 23 minutes

1 package (11 ounces) refrigerated French bread dough
Butter-flavored cooking spray
1 tablespoon olive oil
½ teaspoon dried basil (optional)
1 tablespoon grated Parmesan cheese

1. Preheat oven to 350°F.

2. Place dough roll on cutting board. Cut dough into 12 pieces using serrated knife.

3. Coat 9-inch round baking pan with cooking spray. Brush dough pieces lightly with oil; arrange slices smooth side up almost touching each other in pan. Sprinkle with basil, if desired. Bake 22 to 24 minutes or until rolls are golden and sound hollow when tapped. Remove from oven to wire rack.

4. Lightly spray tops of rolls with cooking spray. Sprinkle with cheese.

Makes 12 serving

Nutrients per Serving (1 roll): Calories: 75, Total Fat: 2 g,
Calories from Fat: 26%, Saturated Fat: 1 g, Cholesterol: <1 mg,
Sodium: 170 mg, Carbohydrate: 11 g, Dietary Fiber: <1 g, Protein: 2 g
Dietary Exchanges: 1 Starch

Black Bean Dip

1 can (15 ounces) low-sodium black beans, undrained
1 clove garlic
¼ cup minced green onions
2 tablespoons minced parsley
¼ cup roasted red pepper or pimientos
1 tablespoon tahini (sesame paste) or olive oil
1 teaspoon chili powder
1 tablespoon *each* lime juice and hot pepper sauce
Assorted fresh vegetables (optional)

Place all ingredients in food processor and process until smooth. Serve with assorted vegetables, if desired. *Makes 10 servings*

Nutrients per Serving (2 tablespoons dip without vegetables): Calories: 37, Total Fat: <1 g, Calories from Fat: 18%, Saturated Fat: 0 g, Cholesterol: 0 mg, Sodium: 109 mg, Carbohydrate: 7 g, Dietary Fiber: 2 g, Protein: 2 g

Dietary Exchanges: ½ Starch

Rice Cake De-Light

4 rice cakes
¼ cup light cream cheese, softened
¼ cup low-calorie fruit preserves

Top rice cakes with cream cheese, then with preserves.

For Rice Cake Treats, top rice cakes with 2 tablespoons smooth peanut butter and 2 small sliced bananas.

Makes 4 servings

Variations: For Summer Fruit Rice Cakes, arrange on top of cakes with cream cheese, 1 can (11 ounces) drained mandarin orange segments, sliced kiwifruit, and ½ cup sliced strawberries.

Favorite recipe from **USA Rice**

Nutrients per Serving (1 rice cake with 1 tablespoon light cream cheese and tablespoon preserves): Calories: 95, Total Fat: 3 g, Calories from Fat: 27%, Saturated Fat: 2 g, Cholesterol: 8 mg, Sodium: 89 mg, Carbohydrate: 15 g, Dietary Fiber: 1 g, Protein: 2 g

Dietary Exchanges: 1 Fruit, ½ Fat

Marinated Artichoke Cheese Toasts

1 jar (8 ounces) marinated artichoke hearts, drained
½ cup (2 ounces) shredded reduced-fat Swiss cheese
⅓ cup finely chopped roasted red peppers
⅓ cup finely chopped celery
1 tablespoon plus 1½ teaspoons reduced-fat mayonnaise
24 melba toast rounds
Paprika

1. Rinse artichokes under cold running water; drain well. Pat dry with paper towels. Finely chop artichokes; place in medium bowl. Add cheese, peppers, celery and mayonnaise; mix well.

2. Spoon artichoke mixture evenly onto melba toast rounds; place on large nonstick baking sheet or broiler pan. Broil 6 inches from heat about 45 seconds or until cheese mixture is hot and bubbly. Sprinkle with paprika. *Makes 12 servings*

Nutrients per Serving (2 toasts): Calories: 57, Total Fat: 1 g, Calories from Fat: 23%, Saturated Fat: 1 g, Cholesterol: 4 mg, Sodium: 65 mg, Carbohydrate: 7 g, Dietary Fiber: 1 g, Protein: 4 g

Dietary Exchanges: ½ Starch

Bubbling Wisconsin Cheese Bread

½ cup (2 ounces) shredded Wisconsin Mozzarella cheese
⅓ cup mayonnaise or salad dressing
⅛ teaspoon garlic powder
⅛ teaspoon onion powder
 1 loaf (16 ounces) French bread, halved lengthwise
⅓ cup grated Wisconsin Parmesan cheese

Preheat oven to 350°F. Combine mozzarella cheese, mayonnaise, garlic powder and onion powder in mixing bowl; mix well (mixture will be very thick). Spread half the mixture over each bread half. Sprinkle half the Parmesan cheese over each half. Bake 20 to 25 minutes or until bubbly and lightly browned.* Cut each half into 8 slices.   *Makes 16 serving*

*To broil, position on rack 4 inches from heat for 3 to 5 minutes.

Favorite recipe from **Wisconsin Milk Marketing Board**

Nutrients per Serving (1 slice (¹⁄₁₆ of loaf)): Calories: 117, Total Fat: 4 g, Calories from Fat: 30%, Saturated Fat: 1 g, Cholesterol: 5 mg, Sodium: 237 mg, Carbohydrate: 16 g, Dietary Fiber: 1 g, Protein: 4 g

Dietary Exchanges: 1 Starch, 1 Fat

Taco Quesadillas

Nonstick cooking spray
½ pound 93% lean ground turkey
¼ cup *each* chopped onion and chopped green bell pepper
½ cup chunky salsa
¾ cup (3 ounces) shredded reduced-fat sharp Cheddar cheese
12 (6-inch) corn tortillas

. Spray medium nonstick skillet with cooking spray. Heat over medium eat. Add turkey, stirring to break up meat; cook until no longer pink. Add nion and bell pepper. Cook until meat begins to brown and vegetables re crisp-tender. Stir in salsa; heat through.

. Heat another medium nonstick skillet over medium heat. Sprinkle tortilla with 1 tablespoon cheese. Top with ⅓ cup turkey mixture; rinkle with 1 tablespoon cheese. Place another tortilla on top of cheese, ressing slightly. Spray top tortilla with cooking spray.

. Place quesadilla, coated side down, in heated skillet. Cook 3 minutes. pray top of tortilla with cooking spray. Carefully flip quesadilla over; cook minutes. Cool slightly; cut into 4 wedges. Repeat with remaining gredients.   *Makes 6 servings*

utrients per Serving (4 wedges): Calories: 224, Total Fat: 8 g, alories from Fat: 29%, Saturated Fat: 3 g, Cholesterol: 26 mg, odium: 365 mg, Carbohydrate: 27 g, Dietary Fiber: 4 g, Protein: 14 g

ietary Exchanges: 2 Starch, 1 Lean Meat, 1 Fat

Mediterranean Bread Braid

Prep Time: 10 minutes • **Bake Time:** 26 minutes
Cool Time: about 1 hour

2 teaspoons dried basil
1 teaspoon dried oregano
½ teaspoon dried rosemary
¼ teaspoon garlic powder
1 package (11 ounces) refrigerated French bread dough
2 ounces olives, pitted and finely chopped (about 16)
2 teaspoons olive oil

1. Preheat oven to 350°F.

2. Combine basil, oregano, rosemary and garlic powder in small bowl. Lightly spray baking sheet with nonstick cooking spray. Unroll dough on baking sheet. Sprinkle evenly with olives and basil mixture. Cut lengthwise into 3 strips. Fold each strip in half lengthwise, creating 3 rope-like strips. Braid bread and tuck ends under slightly.

3. Bake 26 minutes or until bread is golden and sounds hollow when lightly tapped.

4. Cool on cutting board. Brush olive oil over top. Cut diagonally into 12 slices. *Makes 12 servings (1 loaf)*

Tip: Peak flavors are reached by allowing the bread to cool to room temperature.

Nutrients per Serving (1 slice (1/12 of loaf)): Calories: 76, Total Fat: 2 g, Calories from Fat: 25%, Saturated Fat: 1 g, Cholesterol: 0 mg, Sodium: 205 mg, Carbohydrate: 12 g, Dietary Fiber: 1 g, Protein: 2 g
Dietary Exchanges: 1 Starch, ½ Fat

Winter Squash Soup (p. 44)

Open-Face Pear and Waln Breakfast Sandwich (p. 48

Tomato and Turkey Soup
with Pesto (p. 52)

Breakfast Burger (p. 32)

Soups &
Sandwiches

Breakfast Burgers

¾ pound extra-lean ground turkey
½ cup minced red bell pepper
½ cup minced green bell pepper
2 teaspoons dried onion flakes
1 teaspoon dried parsley flakes
½ teaspoon black pepper
Nonstick cooking spray
4 whole wheat English muffins
4 large spinach leaves, stems removed
4 slices soy cheese

1. Mix turkey, bell peppers, onion flakes, parsley flakes and black pepper in large bowl. Shape mixture into 4 patties and spray with nonstick cooking spray.

2. Cook in nonstick skillet over medium heat 7 minutes or until lightly browned on bottom. Turn patties and cook 7 minutes more. Add 2 tablespoons water; cover and cook 3 minutes.

3. Lightly toast English muffins. Place 1 spinach leaf, 1 turkey burger and 1 slice cheese on English muffin half; top with remaining English muffin half. Repeat with remaining burgers. *Makes 4 serving.*

Nutrients per Serving (1 burger): Calories: 300, Total Fat: 6 g, Calories from Fat: 19%, Saturated Fat: 2 g, Cholesterol: 30 mg, Sodium: 576 mg, Carbohydrate: 30 g, Dietary Fiber: 5 g, Protein: 31 g

Dietary Exchanges: 2 Starch, 3 Lean Meat

Mediterranean Pita Sandwiches

1 cup plain fat-free yogurt
1 tablespoon chopped fresh cilantro
2 cloves garlic, minced
1 teaspoon lemon juice
1 can (about 15 ounces) chickpeas, rinsed and drained
1 can (14 ounces) artichoke hearts, rinsed, drained and coarsely chopped
1½ cups thinly sliced cucumber halves (halved lengthwise)
½ cup *each* **shredded carrot and chopped green onions**
4 rounds whole wheat pita bread, cut in half

1. Combine yogurt, cilantro, garlic and lemon juice in small bowl.

2. Combine chickpeas, artichoke hearts, cucumbers, carrot and green onions in medium bowl. Stir in yogurt mixture until well blended.

3. Divide cucumber mixture among pita halves.   *Makes 4 serving*

Nutrients per Serving (2 filled pita halves): Calories: 297, Total Fat: 3 g, Calories from Fat: 9%, Saturated Fat: 1 g, Cholesterol: 1 mg, Sodium: 726 mg, Carbohydrate: 57 g, Dietary Fiber: 9 g, Protein: 15 g

Dietary Exchanges: 3 Starch, 2½ Vegetable, ½ Fat

Asian Ramen Noodle Soup

2 cans (about 14 ounces each) fat-free reduced-sodium chicken broth
4 ounces boneless pork loin, cut into thin strips
¾ cup thinly sliced mushrooms
½ cup firm tofu, cut into ¼-inch cubes (optional)
3 tablespoons *each* white vinegar and sherry
1 tablespoon reduced-sodium soy sauce
½ teaspoon ground red pepper
2 ounces uncooked low-fat ramen noodles
1 egg, beaten
¼ cup finely chopped green onions, green tops only

1. Bring chicken broth to a boil in large saucepan over high heat; add pork, mushrooms and tofu, if desired. Reduce heat to medium-low; simmer, covered, 5 minutes. Stir in vinegar, sherry, soy sauce and pepper.

2. Return broth mixture to a boil over high heat; stir in ramen noodles. Cook, stirring occasionally, 5 to 7 minutes or until noodles are tender. Slowly stir in egg and green onions; remove from heat. Ladle soup into individual bowls.   *Makes 4 serving*

Nutrients per Serving (¾ cup): Calories: 148, Total Fat: 4 g, Calories from Fat: 24%, Saturated Fat: 1 g, Cholesterol: 66 mg, Sodium: 269 mg, Carbohydrate: 15 g, Dietary Fiber: 1 g, Protein: 10 g

Dietary Exchanges: ½ Starch, 1 Vegetable, 1½ Lean Meat

Italian Tomato Soup

½ pound lean ground beef
½ cup chopped onion
1 clove garlic, minced
1 can (28 ounces) tomatoes, undrained, cut into pieces
1 can (15 ounces) white kidney beans, drained, rinsed
¾ cup HEINZ® Tomato Ketchup
½ cup thinly sliced carrots
1 teaspoon dried basil leaves
¼ teaspoon salt

In medium saucepan, brown beef, onion and garlic; drain excess fat. Add tomatoes with juices and remaining ingredients. Cover; simmer 15 minutes.

Makes 4 to 6 servings (about 6 cups)

Nutrients per Serving (1½ cups): Calories: 296, Total Fat: 8 g, Calories from Fat: 24%, Saturated Fat: 3 g, Cholesterol: 35 mg, Sodium: 1,378 mg, Carbohydrate: 40 g, Dietary Fiber: 9 g, Protein: 18 g

Dietary Exchanges: 2 Starch, 2 Vegetable, 2 Lean Meat

Caribbean Jerk Chicken Open-Faced Sandwiches

4 (4-ounce) boneless skinless chicken breasts
2 small yellow or red bell peppers, seeded and quartered
⅓ cup hickory-flavored barbecue sauce
2 teaspoons Caribbean jerk seasoning
4 tablespoons reduced-fat mayonnaise
4 slices whole wheat or whole-grain bread, lightly toasted
1 cup packed spinach leaves or arugula leaves

1. Prepare grill for direct cooking. Place chicken and bell peppers on grid over medium coals.

2. Combine barbecue sauce and jerk seasoning; brush half of mixture over chicken and peppers.

3. Grill, covered, 5 minutes. Turn; brush remaining sauce mixture over chicken and peppers. Grill 4 to 6 minutes or until chicken is no longer pink in center and peppers are tender.

4. Spread 1 tablespoon mayonnaise onto each piece of toast; top with spinach, pepper quarters and chicken.   *Makes 4 servings*

Nutrients per Serving (1 sandwich (1 slice bread, 1 chicken breast and 2 bell pepper quarters)): Calories: 251, Total Fat: 7 g, Calories from Fat: 25%, Saturated Fat: 2 g, Cholesterol: 43 mg, Sodium: 709 mg, Carbohydrate: 26 g, Dietary Fiber: 3 g, Protein: 21 g

Dietary Exchanges: 1 Starch, 1 Vegetable, 3 Lean Meat

Minted Melon Soup

1 cup water
1 tablespoon sugar
1½ cups fresh mint, including stems
2 fresh basil leaves
1½ cups diced cantaloupe
4 teaspoons lemon juice, divided
1½ cups diced seeded watermelon
4 fresh mint sprigs (optional)

1. Combine water and sugar in small saucepan; mix well. Bring to a boil over medium heat. Add mint and basil; simmer 10 minutes or until reduced by two-thirds. Remove from heat; cover and let stand at least 2 hours or until cool. Strain mint syrup; set aside.

2. Place cantaloupe in food processor or blender; process until smooth. Add 2 tablespoons mint syrup and 2 teaspoons lemon juice; process until well mixed. Pour into airtight container. Cover and refrigerate until cold. Repeat procedure with watermelon, 2 teaspoons mint syrup and remaining 2 teaspoons lemon juice. Discard any remaining mint syrup.

3. To serve, simultaneously pour ¼ cup of each melon soup, side by side, into serving bowl. Garnish with 1 mint sprig. Repeat with remaining soup.

Makes 4 servings

Nutrients per Serving (½ cup): Calories: 48, Total Fat: <1 g, Calories from Fat: 7%, Saturated Fat: 0 g, Cholesterol: 0 mg, Sodium: 7 mg, Carbohydrate: 11 g, Dietary Fiber: 1 g, Protein: 1 g

Dietary Exchanges: 1 Fruit

Beef Burgers with Corn Salsa

½ cup frozen corn
½ cup peeled, seeded and chopped tomato
1 can (4 ounces) diced green chiles, divided
1 tablespoon chopped fresh cilantro *or* 1 teaspoon dried cilantro
1 tablespoon vinegar
1 teaspoon olive oil
¼ cup fine dry bread crumbs
3 tablespoons fat-free (skim) milk
¼ teaspoon garlic powder
12 ounces 95% lean ground beef

1. Prepare corn according to package directions, omitting salt; drain. Combine corn, tomato, 2 tablespoons green chiles, cilantro, vinegar and oil in small bowl. Cover and refrigerate.

2. Preheat broiler. Combine bread crumbs, remaining green chiles, milk and garlic powder in medium bowl. Add beef; blend well. Shape mixture into four ¾-inch-thick patties. Place on broiler pan. Broil 4 inches from heat 6 minutes. Turn and broil 6 to 8 minutes or until beef is no longer pink in center. Spoon salsa over patties. *Makes 4 servings*

Nutrients per Serving (1 burger with 1 tablespoon plus 2 teaspoons salsa): Calories: 180, Total Fat: 6 g, Calories from Fat: 30%, Saturated Fat: 2 g, Cholesterol: 33 mg, Sodium: 101 mg, Carbohydrate: 13 g, Dietary Fiber: 2 g, Protein: 19 g

Dietary Exchanges: ½ Starch, 1 Vegetable, 2½ Lean Meat, 1 Fat

Winter Squash Soup

1 tablespoon low-fat vegetable oil spread
1 tablespoon minced shallot or onion
2 cloves garlic, minced
3 fresh thyme sprigs
1 pinch dried rosemary
2 packages (10 ounces each) frozen winter (butternut) squash, thawed
1 cup fat-free reduced-sodium chicken broth
3 tablespoons fat-free (skim) milk
Fat-free sour cream (optional)

1. Melt vegetable oil spread in medium saucepan over medium heat. Add shallot, garlic, thyme and rosemary. Cook and stir 2 to 3 minutes or until shallot is tender. Add squash and chicken broth; bring to a boil. Add milk; stir until blended.

2. Remove thyme sprigs from soup. Transfer soup to blender or food processor; blend until smooth. (Add additional liquid to make soup thinner, if desired.) Top with dollop of sour cream.   *Makes 4 servings*

Nutrients per Serving (1 cup): Calories: 116, Total Fat: 2 g, Calories from Fat: 16%, Saturated Fat: <1 g, Cholesterol: <1 mg, Sodium: 135 mg, Carbohydrate: 22 g, Dietary Fiber: 2 g, Protein: 5 g

Dietary Exchanges: 4 Vegetable, ½ Fat

Chicken in a Pita

½ cup light mayonnaise or salad dressing
1 tablespoon low-sodium soy sauce
¼ teaspoon ground ginger
1 tablespoon reduced-fat peanut butter
1 cup chopped, cooked, boneless skinless chicken breast
½ cup snow peas, cut into halves
½ cup chopped red or yellow bell peppers
1 tablespoon roasted peanuts
3 whole pita breads, cut into halves

Mix mayonnaise, soy sauce, ginger and peanut butter together until well blended. Add chicken and vegetables; refrigerate 1 to 4 hours. Stir in peanuts and spoon into pita pockets.   *Makes 6 pita halves*

Favorite recipe from **Wheat Foods Council**

Nutrients per Serving (1 filled pita half): Calories: 211, Total Fat: 8 g, Calories from Fat: 36%, Saturated Fat: 1 g, Cholesterol: 25 mg, Sodium: 401 mg, Carbohydrate: 23 g, Dietary Fiber: 1 g, Protein: 11 g

Dietary Exchanges: 1½ Starch, 1 Lean Meat, 1 Fat

Grilled Veggie Burgers

4 frozen veggie burgers
4 slices sweet onion, such as Vidalia
4 slices reduced-fat Swiss cheese

1. Spray grid lightly with nonstick cooking spray. Prepare grill for direct cooking.

2. Place burgers and onion slices on grill. Grill 5 minutes or until burgers are heated through and onion is soft, turning once.

3. Place cheese slices on burgers; top with onion slices. Serve immediately.

Makes 4 servings

Nutrients per Serving (1 burger with 1 cheese slice and onion slice):
Calories: 215, Total Fat: 5 g, Calories from Fat: 24%, Saturated Fat: 2 g,
Cholesterol: 15 mg, Sodium: 410 mg, Carbohydrate: 8 g, Dietary Fiber: 3 g,
Protein: 32 g

Dietary Exchanges: 4 Lean Meat

Open-Face Pear and Walnut Breakfast Sandwiches

2 pears, peeled and chopped
½ cup unsweetened applesauce
3 tablespoons chopped walnuts
2 tablespoons sucralose
½ teaspoon ground cinnamon
¼ teaspoon ground nutmeg
4 slices multi-grain bread
⅓ cup finely shredded Swiss cheese
Chopped dried cranberries (optional)

1. Preheat oven to 425°F. Combine pears, applesauce, walnuts, sucralose, cinnamon and nutmeg in small bowl.

2. Toast bread; top evenly with pear-walnut mixture. Place on nonstick baking sheet. Top each slice evenly with shredded Swiss cheese; bake 8 minutes.

3. Garnish with 1 teaspoon cranberries.   *Makes 4 serving*

Nutrients per Serving (1 slice bread with ¼ cup topping): Calories: 171, Total Fat: 5 g, Calories from Fat: 16%, Saturated Fat: <1 g, Cholesterol: 3 mg, Sodium: 139 mg, Carbohydrate: 303 g, Dietary Fiber: 5 g, Protein: 6 g

Dietary Exchanges: 1 Starch, 1 Fruit, 1 Fat

Wild Rice Soup

½ **cup lentils**
1 **package (6 ounces) long grain and wild rice blend**
1 **can (about 14 ounces) vegetable broth**
1 **package (10 ounces) frozen mixed vegetables**
1 **cup fat-free (skim) milk**
2 **slices (1 ounce each) reduced-fat American cheese, cut into pieces**

1. Rinse and sort lentils, discarding any debris or blemished lentils. Place lentils in small saucepan; cover with about 3 cups water. Bring to a boil; reduce heat to low. Simmer, covered, 5 minutes. Let stand, covered, 1 hour. Drain and rinse lentils.

2. Cook rice according to package directions in medium saucepan. Add lentils and remaining ingredients. Bring to a boil; reduce heat to low. Simmer, uncovered, 20 minutes. *Makes 6 serving*

Nutrients per Serving (1 bowl of soup (⅙ of total recipe)): Calories: 231, Total Fat: 3 g, Calories from Fat: 10%, Saturated Fat: 1 g, Cholesterol: 6 mg, Sodium: 585 mg, Carbohydrate: 41 g, Dietary Fiber: 7 g, Protein: 13 g

Dietary Exchanges: 3 Starch, ½ Fat

Tomato and Turkey Soup with Pesto

1 cup uncooked rotini pasta
1 can (10¾ ounces) condensed reduced-sodium tomato soup, undiluted
1 cup fat-free (skim) milk
2 cups (8 ounces) frozen Italian-style vegetables
2 tablespoons prepared pesto
1 cup coarsely chopped skinless cooked turkey
2 tablespoons grated Parmesan cheese

1. Cook pasta according to package directions, omitting salt; drain. Set aside.

2. Meanwhile, combine soup, milk, vegetables and pesto in medium saucepan. Bring to a boil over medium heat; reduce heat to low. Simmer, partially covered, 10 minutes or until vegetables are tender. Add pasta and turkey. Cook 3 minutes or until heated through. Sprinkle with cheese just before serving. *Makes 4 serving.*

Nutrients per Serving (1½ cups soup with 1½ teaspoons Parmesan cheese): Calories: 285, Total Fat: 7 g, Calories from Fat: 21%, Saturated Fat: 2 g, Cholesterol: 28 mg, Sodium: 462 mg, Carbohydrate: 38 g, Dietary Fiber: 3 g, Protein: 18 g

Dietary Exchanges: 2 Starch, 1 Vegetable, 2 Lean Meat

Curried Creamy Sweet Potato Soup

4 cups water
1 pound sweet potatoes, peeled and cut into 1-inch cubes
1 tablespoon plus 1 teaspoon butter or margarine, divided
2 cups finely chopped yellow onions
2 cups fat-free (skim) milk, divided
¾ teaspoon curry powder
½ teaspoon salt
   Dash ground red pepper (optional)

1. Bring water to a boil in large saucepan over high heat. Add potatoes; return to a boil. Reduce heat to medium-low and simmer, uncovered, 15 minutes or until potatoes are tender.

2. Meanwhile, heat medium nonstick skillet over medium-high heat until hot. Coat with nonstick cooking spray; add 1 teaspoon butter and tilt skillet to coat bottom. Add onions; cook 8 minutes or until tender and golden.

3. Drain potatoes; place in blender with onions, 1 cup milk, curry powder, salt and ground red pepper. Blend until completely smooth. Return potato mixture to saucepan and stir in remaining 1 cup milk. Cook 5 minutes over medium-high heat or until heated through. Remove from heat and stir in remaining 1 tablespoon butter. *Makes 4 servings*

Nutrients per Serving (¾ cup): Calories: 201, Total Fat: 5 g, Calories from Fat: 20%, Saturated Fat: 3 g, Cholesterol: 13 mg, Sodium: 406 mg, Carbohydrate: 35 g, Dietary Fiber: 4 g, Protein: 7 g

Dietary Exchanges: 2 Starch, 1 Vegetable, 1 Fat

Roast Beef and Feta Pitas with Cucumber Sauce

Prep Time: 15 minutes

¼ **cup (1 ounce) crumbled feta cheese**
⅓ **cup reduced-fat sour cream**
1 **medium cucumber, peeled, seeded and coarsely shredded (1 cup shredded)**
2 **tablespoons diced red onion**
1½ **teaspoons lemon juice**
¼ **teaspoon black pepper**
4 **(6½-inch) rounds whole wheat pita bread, cut in half and warmed**
8 **fresh spinach leaves, washed and stems removed**
12 **ounces deli-sliced lean roast beef**
8 *each* **fresh tomato slices and red onion slices**

1. Combine cheese, sour cream, cucumber, onion, lemon juice and pepper in medium bowl. Set aside.

2. Line insides of pita pockets with spinach. Add roast beef, tomato and onion. Serve with sour cream mixture. *Makes 4 servings*

Note: This sauce would also be good drizzled over a sliced tomato salad and grilled or broiled fish.

Tip: Two sandwich halves may easily fit into your meal plan. If eating both halves is going to put you way above your carb, sodium and other nutrient limits, however, wrap up one of the halves and save it for another meal or snack.

Nutrients per Serving (1 sandwich (2 filled halves) with ¼ cup sauce): Calories: 358, Total Fat: 8 g, Calories from Fat: 19%, Saturated Fat: 4 g, Cholesterol: 49 mg, Sodium: 1,109 mg, Carbohydrate: 49 g, Dietary Fiber: 7 g, Protein: 26 g

Dietary Exchanges: 2½ Starch, 2 Vegetable, 2 Lean Meat

Double Pea Soup

1 tablespoon vegetable oil
1 large white onion, finely chopped
3 cloves garlic, finely chopped
2 cups water
2 cups dried split peas
1 bay leaf
1 teaspoon ground mustard
1½ cups frozen green peas
1 teaspoon salt
¼ teaspoon black pepper
     Fat-free sour cream (optional)

1. Heat oil in large saucepan or Dutch oven over medium-high heat until hot. Add onion; cook 5 minutes or until onion is tender, stirring occasionally. Add garlic; cook and stir 2 minutes.

2. Stir water, split peas, bay leaf and mustard into saucepan. Bring to a boil over high heat. Cover and reduce heat to medium-low. Simmer 45 minutes or until split peas are tender, stirring occasionally.

3. Stir green peas, salt and pepper into saucepan; cover. Cook 10 minutes or until green peas are tender. Remove bay leaf; discard. Process small batches in blender or food processor until smooth.

4. Top each serving with sour cream before serving, if desired.

Makes 6 servings

Note: For a smoky flavor, add a chipotle pepper during the last 5 minutes of cooking.

Nutrients per Serving (⅙ of total recipe): Calories: 290, Total Fat: 3 g, Calories from Fat: 10%, Saturated Fat: <1 g, Cholesterol: 0 mg, Sodium: 401 mg, Carbohydrate: 48 g, Dietary Fiber: 5 g, Protein: 19 g

Dietary Exchanges: 3 Starch, ½ Vegetable, 1 Lean Meat

Beef & Bean Burrito (p. 82)

Yankee Pot Roast (p. 70)

Citrus Ginger Teriyaki
Steak (p. 76)

Veggie-Beef Hash (p. 72)

Zesty Beef Dishes

Chili Beef and Corn Casserole

Nonstick cooking spray
¾ **pound 96% lean ground beef**
¼ **cup reduced-sodium salsa**
2 **teaspoons chili powder**
1½ **teaspoons ground cumin**
2 **cups frozen corn kernels, thawed**
2 **ounces chopped collard greens, about ½-inch pieces (1 cup packed)**
½ **cup fat-free sour cream**
¼ **cup (1 ounce) shredded reduced-fat sharp Cheddar cheese**

1. Preheat oven 350°F.

2. Coat 12-inch nonstick skillet with cooking spray. Brown beef 6 to 8 minutes over medium-high heat, stirring to break up meat. Drain fat. Add salsa, chili powder and cumin; cook and stir 1 minute. Remove from heat.

3. Coat 8-inch square baking pan with cooking spray. Place corn and collard greens in bottom of pan; toss to blend. Spoon beef mixture evenly over vegetables; cover tightly with foil. Bake 25 minutes or until greens are tender.

4. Top each serving with 2 tablespoons sour cream and 1 tablespoon shredded cheese.
Makes 4 servings

Nutrients per Serving (1 cup): Calories: 240, Total Fat: 5 g, Calories from Fat: 20%, Saturated Fat: 2 g, Cholesterol: 60 mg, Sodium: 249 mg, Carbohydrate: 25 g, Dietary Fiber: 3 g, Protein: 25 g
Dietary Exchanges: 1½ Starch, 3 Lean Meat

Beef & Vegetable Skillet

Prep and Cook Time: 30 minutes

1¼ pounds boneless beef top sirloin steak, cut ¾ inch thick
2 teaspoons dark sesame oil
2 garlic cloves, minced
1 medium red bell pepper, cut into thin strips
2 tablespoons reduced-sodium soy sauce
2 tablespoons water
3 cups coarsely chopped fresh spinach
½ cup sliced green onions
3 tablespoons ketchup
1 tablespoon reduced-sodium soy sauce
2 cups hot cooked rice, prepared without butter or salt

1. Cut beef steak lengthwise in half and then crosswise into ¼-inch strips. Toss with sesame oil and garlic.

2. Heat large nonstick skillet over medium-high heat until hot. Add beef (½ at a time); stir-fry 1 to 2 minutes or until outside surface is no longer pink. Remove from skillet.

3. In same skillet, add bell pepper, 2 tablespoons soy sauce and water. Cook 2 to 3 minutes or until pepper is crisp-tender. Add spinach and green onions; cook until spinach is just wilted. Stir in ketchup, 1 tablespoon soy sauce and beef; heat through. Serve over rice.

Makes 4 servings

Favorite recipe from **National Cattlemen's Beef Association on behalf of The Beef Checkoff**

Nutrients per Serving (¼ of total recipe): Calories: 334, Total Fat: 9 g, Calories from Fat: 24%, Saturated Fat: 3 g, Cholesterol: 62 mg, Sodium: 688 mg, Carbohydrate: 25 g, Dietary Fiber: 2 g, Protein: 36 g

Dietary Exchanges: 1 Starch, 2 Vegetable, 4 Lean Meat

Beef Patties with Blue Cheese & Veggies

1 pound 95% lean ground beef
2 tablespoons steak sauce
½ teaspoon salt, divided
  Nonstick cooking spray
¼ cup (1 ounce) crumbled blue cheese
1 teaspoon olive oil
8 ounces yellow squash, cut in half lengthwise, then
  crosswise into ½-inch slices
1 medium onion, cut into eight wedges
¼ cup finely chopped parsley

1. Combine beef, steak sauce and ¼ teaspoon salt in small bowl; mix well. Shape into 4 patties.

2. Spray large nonstick skillet with cooking spray; heat over medium-high heat until hot. Cook patties 4 minutes. Reduce heat to medium. Turn patties; cook 3 to 4 minutes longer or until no longer pink in center (160°F). Remove from skillet to plate. Sprinkle each patty with 1 tablespoon cheese; cover with foil to keep warm.

3. Add oil to same skillet. Add squash and onion; cook and stir 5 to 6 minutes over medium-high heat or until edges of vegetables begin to brown; sprinkle with remaining ¼ teaspoon salt. Spoon vegetables over beef; sprinkle evenly with parsley.   *Makes 4 servings*

Nutrients per Serving (1 patty plus ½ cup vegetables and 1 tablespoon cheese): Calories: 219, Total Fat: 9 g, Calories from Fat: 37%, Saturated Fat: 4 g, Cholesterol: 72 mg, Sodium: 576 mg, Carbohydrate: 6 g, Dietary Fiber: 1 g, Protein: 27 g

Dietary Exchanges: 1 Vegetable, 3 Lean Meat

Tex-Mex Flank Steak Salad

½ beef flank steak (about 6 ounces)
½ teaspoon Mexican seasoning blend or chili powder
⅛ teaspoon salt
Olive oil cooking spray
4 cups packaged mixed salad greens
1 can (11 ounces) mandarin orange sections, drained
2 tablespoons green taco sauce

1. Cut flank steak lengthwise in half, then crosswise into thin strips. Combine beef slices, Mexican seasoning and salt in medium bowl.

2. Lightly spray large nonstick skillet with cooking spray. Heat over medium-high heat. Add steak strips. Cook and stir 1 to 2 minutes or until desired doneness.

3. Toss together greens and orange sections. Arrange on serving plates. Top with warm steak. Drizzle with taco sauce. *Makes 2 servings*

Nutrients per Serving (½ of total recipe): Calories: 240, Total Fat: 7 g, Calories from Fat: 25%, Saturated Fat: 3 g, Cholesterol: 37 mg, Sodium: 388 mg, Carbohydrate: 21 g, Dietary Fiber: 2 g, Protein: 25 g

Dietary Exchanges: 1 Fruit, 2 Vegetable, 2 Lean Meat

Sirloin with Sweet Caramelized Onions

Nonstick cooking spray
1 medium onion, very thinly sliced
1 boneless beef top sirloin steak (about 1 pound)
¼ cup water
2 tablespoons Worcestershire sauce
1 tablespoon sugar

1. Lightly coat 12-inch skillet with cooking spray; heat over high heat until hot. Add onion; cook and stir 4 minutes or until browned. Remove from skillet and set aside. Wipe out skillet with paper towel.

2. Coat same skillet with cooking spray; heat until hot. Add beef; cook 10 to 13 minutes for medium-rare to medium, turning once. Remove from heat and transfer to cutting board; let stand 3 minutes before slicing.

3. Meanwhile, return skillet to high heat until hot; add onion, water, Worcestershire sauce and sugar. Cook 30 to 45 seconds or until most liquid has evaporated.

4. Thinly slice beef on the diagonal and serve with onions.

Makes 4 servings

Nutrients per Serving (¼ of total recipe): Calories: 159, Total Fat: 5 g, Calories from Fat: 28%, Saturated Fat: 2 g, Cholesterol: 60 mg, Sodium: 118 mg, Carbohydrate: 7 g, Dietary Fiber: 1 g, Protein: 21 g

Dietary Exchanges: 3 Lean Meat

Bolognese Sauce & Penne Pasta

  8 ounces 95% lean ground beef
  ⅓ cup chopped onion
  1 clove garlic, minced
  1 can (8 ounces) tomato sauce
  ⅓ cup chopped carrot
  ¼ cup water
  2 tablespoons red wine
  1 teaspoon dried Italian seasoning
  1½ cups hot cooked penne pasta
  Chopped fresh parsley

1. Brown beef, onion and garlic in medium saucepan over medium-high heat 6 to 8 minutes, stirring to break up meat. Drain fat.

2. Add tomato sauce, carrot, water, wine and Italian seasoning. Bring to a boil. Reduce heat and simmer 15 minutes. Serve sauce over pasta. Sprinkle with parsley.   *Makes 2 servings*

Nutrients per Serving (¾ cup cooked pasta with half of sauce): Calories: 292, Total Fat: 5 g, Calories from Fat: 14%, Saturated Fat: 2 g, Cholesterol: 45 mg, Sodium: 734 mg, Carbohydrate: 40 g, Dietary Fiber: 4 g, Protein: 21 g

Dietary Exchanges: 2 Starch, 1 Vegetable, 2 Lean Meat

Cajun-Style Beef and Beans

Prep Time: 35 minutes (includes time for cooking rice)
Bake Time: 25 to 30 minutes • **Stand Time:** 5 minutes

1 pound 95% lean ground beef
¾ cup chopped onion
2½ cups cooked brown rice
1 can (16 ounces) kidney beans, rinsed and drained
1 can (14½ ounces) stewed tomatoes, undrained
2 tablespoons Cajun seasoning
¾ cup (3 ounces) shredded reduced-fat Cheddar cheese

1. Preheat oven to 350°F. Brown beef and onion in large skillet over medium-high heat 6 to 8 minutes, stirring to break up meat. Drain fat.

2. Combine beef mixture, cooked rice, beans, tomatoes with juice and Cajun seasoning in 2- to 2½-quart casserole. Bake, covered, 25 to 30 minutes, stirring once during baking. Remove from oven; sprinkle with cheese. Let stand, covered, 5 minutes before serving.   *Makes 6 servings*

Nutrients per Serving (1½ cups): Calories: 344, Total Fat: 9 g, Calories from Fat: 23%, Saturated Fat: 4 g, Cholesterol: 54 mg, Sodium: 642 mg, Carbohydrate: 39 g, Dietary Fiber: 8 g, Protein: 27 g

Dietary Exchanges: 2 Starch, 2 Vegetable, 2½ Lean Meat

Yankee Pot Roast

Prep and Cook Time: 3 hours to 3½ hours

> 1 boneless beef chuck pot roast (arm, shoulder or blade), about 2½ pounds
> ⅓ cup all-purpose flour
> ¾ teaspoon salt
> ¾ teaspoon pepper
> 1 tablespoon vegetable oil
> 1 can (14 to 14½ ounces) beef broth
> ½ cup dry red wine
> 1½ teaspoons dried thyme leaves, crushed
> 2 packages (16 ounces each) frozen stew vegetable stew mixture (such as potatoes, carrots, celery and onion)

1. Combine flour, salt and pepper. Lightly coat beef in 2 tablespoons of flour mixture. Heat oil in large stockpot over medium heat until hot. Place beef pot roast in stockpot; brown evenly. Drain fat.

2. Combine beef broth, red wine, thyme and remaining flour mixture; add to stockpot and bring to a boil. Reduce heat; cover tightly and simmer 2 hours. Add vegetables to stockpot; continue simmering 30 to 45 minutes or until pot roast and vegetables are fork-tender.

3. Remove pot roast and vegetables; keep warm. Skim fat from cooking liquid, if necessary.

4. Carve pot roast into thin slices. Serve with vegetables and gravy.

Makes 6 servings

Favorite recipe from **National Cattlemen's Beef Association on behalf of The Beef Checkoff**

Nutrients per Serving (⅙ of total recipe): Calories: 363, Total Fat: 10 g, Calories from Fat: 25%, Saturated Fat: 3 g, Cholesterol: 71 mg, Sodium: 735 mg, Carbohydrate: 25 g, Dietary Fiber: 1 g, Protein: 39 g

Dietary Exchanges: ½ Starch, 3½ Vegetable, 4½ Lean Meat

Veggie-Beef Hash

Nonstick cooking spray
4 ounces cooked roast beef, trimmed of all fat, finely chopped
1½ cups frozen seasoning blend*
1 cup shredded potatoes
½ cup shredded carrots
1 egg white *or* 2 tablespoons liquid egg white
½ teaspoon dried rosemary
½ teaspoon black pepper
½ cup reduced-sodium salsa (optional)

Seasoning blend is a combination of finely chopped onion, celery, green and red bell peppers and parsley flakes that can be found in the supermarket frozen-foods aisle. Frozen or fresh sliced bell peppers can be substituted.

1. Lightly spray nonstick skillet with cooking spray; set aside.

2. Combine beef, seasoning blend, potatoes, carrots, egg white, rosemary and black pepper in large bowl. Scoop beef mixture into skillet over medium-high heat, pressing down firmly to form large cake. Cook 4 minutes or until browned, pressing down on cake with spatula several times. Flip cake. Cook 4 minutes or until lightly browned and heated through. Serve with salsa.   *Makes 2 servings*

Nutrients per Serving (½ of total recipe): Calories: 297, Total Fat: 9 g, Calories from Fat: 21%, Saturated Fat: 2 g, Cholesterol: 29 mg, Sodium: 378 mg, Carbohydrate: 33 g, Dietary Fiber: 5 g, Protein: 22 g
Dietary Exchanges: 2 Starch, 2 Lean Meat, 1 Fat

Fragrant Beef with Garlic Sauce

1 boneless beef top sirloin steak (about 1¼ pounds)
⅓ cup reduced-sodium teriyaki sauce
10 large cloves garlic, peeled
½ cup fat-free reduced-sodium beef broth
4 cups hot cooked rice (optional)

1. Place beef in large resealable storage bag. Pour teriyaki sauce over beef. Seal bag and turn to coat. Marinate in refrigerator at least 30 minutes or up to 4 hours.

2. Combine garlic and broth in small saucepan. Bring to a boil over high heat. Reduce heat to medium. Simmer, uncovered, 5 minutes. Cover and simmer 8 to 9 minutes until garlic is softened. Transfer to blender or food processor; process until smooth.

3. Meanwhile, drain beef; reserve marinade. Place beef on rack of broiler pan. Brush with half of reserved marinade. Broil 5 to 6 inches from heat 6 minutes. Turn beef over; brush with remaining marinade. Broil 6 minutes more.*

4. Slice beef thinly; serve with garlic sauce and rice, if desired.

Makes 4 servings

Broiling time is for medium-rare doneness. Adjust time for desired doneness.

Nutrients per Serving (¼ of total recipe (without rice)): Calories: 212, Total Fat: 6 g, Calories from Fat: 24%, Saturated Fat: 2 g, Cholesterol: 67 mg, Sodium: 688 mg, Carbohydrate: 6 g, Dietary Fiber: <1 g, Protein: 33 g

Dietary Exchanges: 4 Lean Meat

Vegetable Spaghetti Sauce with Meatballs

1½ cups sliced fresh mushrooms
½ cup chopped onion plus 2 tablespoons finely chopped onion, divided
½ cup *each* chopped carrot and chopped green bell pepper
2 cloves garlic, minced
2 cans (14½ ounces each) no-salt-added stewed tomatoes, undrained
1 can (6 ounces) no-salt-added tomato paste
2½ teaspoons dried Italian seasoning, divided
½ teaspoon salt
¼ teaspoon black pepper
1 egg white
2 tablespoons fine dry bread crumbs
8 ounces 95% lean ground beef
4 cups hot cooked spaghetti

1. Preheat oven to 375°F. Coat large saucepan with nonstick cooking spray; heat over medium heat. Add mushrooms, ½ cup onion, carrot, bell pepper and garlic. Cook and stir 4 to 5 minutes or until vegetables are tender. Stir in stewed tomatoes with juice, tomato paste, 2 teaspoons Italian seasoning, salt and black pepper. Bring to a boil over medium-high heat. Reduce heat to medium-low. Cover and simmer 20 minutes, stirring occasionally.

2. Combine egg white, bread crumbs, remaining 2 tablespoons onion and remaining ½ teaspoon Italian seasoning in medium bowl. Add beef; mix until well blended. Shape into 16 meatballs. Place in 11×7-inch baking pan. Bake 18 to 20 minutes or until beef is no longer pink. Drain on paper towels.

3. Stir meatballs into sauce. Return sauce to a boil; reduce heat. Simmer, uncovered, about 10 minutes more or until sauce thickens slightly, stirring occasionally. Serve over spaghetti. *Makes 4 servings*

Nutrients per Serving (¼ of total recipe): Calories: 341, Total Fat: 5 g, Calories from Fat: 13%, Saturated Fat: 2 g, Cholesterol: 25 mg, Sodium: 381 mg, Carbohydrate: 56 g, Dietary Fiber: 7 g, Protein: 21 g

Dietary Exchanges: 3½ Starch, 3 Vegetable, 1½ Lean Meat

Citrus Ginger Teriyaki Steak

Prep and Cook Time: 30 minutes • **Marinate Time:** 30 minutes

1 boneless beef top sirloin steak, cut 1 inch thick (about 1 pound)
½ cup water

Marinade & Sauce:
½ cup prepared teriyaki marinade and sauce
⅓ cup orange marmalade
2 tablespoons creamy peanut butter
1 tablespoon finely chopped ginger
3 large garlic cloves, crushed
2 teaspoons dark sesame oil

1. Combine marinade ingredients in small saucepan over medium heat, whisking just until blended. Remove from heat. Place steak and ⅓ cup marinade mixture in plastic bag; turn steak to coat. Close bag securely and marinate in refrigerator 30 minutes, turning once. Reserve remaining marinade mixture for sauce.

2. Remove steak from marinade; discard marinade. Place steak on rack in broiler pan so surface of beef is 3 to 4 inches from heat. Broil steak 16 to 21 minutes for medium rare to medium doneness, turning once.

3. Meanwhile add water to reserved sauce in small saucepan; bring to a boil. Reduce heat and simmer 12 to 15 minutes or until slightly thickened, stirring occasionally.

4. Carve steak into slices. Serve steak with sauce.   *Makes 4 servings*

Favorite recipe from **National Cattlemen's Beef Association on behalf of The Beef Checkoff**

Nutrients per Serving (¼ pound steak with about 3 tablespoons of remaining marinade): Calories: 295, Total Fat: 10 g, Calories from Fat: 31%, Saturated Fat: 3 g, Cholesterol: 50 mg, Sodium: 1118 mg, Carbohydrate: 20 g, Dietary Fiber: 1 g, Protein: 30 g

Dietary Exchanges: 1½ Starch, 3½ Lean Meat

Thai Beef Salad

½ beef flank steak (about 8 ounces)
¼ cup reduced-sodium soy sauce
2 jalapeño peppers,* finely chopped
2 tablespoons packed brown sugar
1 clove garlic, minced
½ cup lime juice
6 green onions, thinly sliced
4 carrots, diagonally cut into thin slices
½ cup finely chopped fresh cilantro
4 romaine lettuce leaves

*Jalapeño peppers can sting and irritate the skin, so wear rubber gloves when handling peppers and do not touch your eyes.

1. Place flank steak in resealable food storage bag. Combine soy sauce, jalapeños, brown sugar and garlic in small bowl; mix well. Pour mixture over flank steak.

2. Close bag securely; turn to coat steak. Marinate in refrigerator 2 hours.

3. Preheat broiler. Drain steak; discard marinade. Place steak on rack of broiler pan. Broil 4 inches from heat 13 to 18 minutes for medium rare to medium or until desired doneness, turning once. Remove from heat; let stand 15 minutes.

4. Thinly slice steak across grain. Toss with lime juice, green onions, carrots and cilantro in large bowl. Serve salad immediately on lettuce leaves. *Makes 4 servings*

Nutrients per Serving (1 cup salad with 1 lettuce leaf): Calories: 141, Total Fat: 4 g, Calories from Fat: 26%, Saturated Fat: 2 g, Cholesterol: 27 mg, Sodium: 238 mg, Carbohydrate: 14 g, Dietary Fiber: 3 g, Protein: 13 g

Dietary Exchanges: 2 Vegetable, 1½ Lean Meat

Baked Pasta Casserole

1½ cups (3 ounces) uncooked wagon wheel or rotelle pasta
3 ounces 95% lean ground beef
2 tablespoons chopped onion
2 tablespoons chopped green bell pepper
1 clove garlic, minced
½ cup fat-free spaghetti sauce
Dash black pepper
2 tablespoons shredded Italian-style mozzarella and Parmesan cheese blend
Peperoncini (optional)

1. Preheat oven to 350°F. Cook pasta according to package directions, omitting salt; drain. Return pasta to saucepan.

2. Meanwhile, heat medium nonstick skillet over medium-high heat. Add beef, onion, bell pepper and garlic; cook and stir 3 to 4 minutes or until beef is no longer pink and vegetables are crisp-tender. Drain.

3. Add beef mixture, spaghetti sauce and black pepper to pasta in saucepan; mix well. Spoon mixture into 1-quart baking dish. Sprinkle with cheese.

4. Bake 15 minutes or until heated through. Serve with peperoncini, if desired.   *Makes 2 servings*

Note: To make ahead, assemble casserole as directed above through step 3. Cover and refrigerate several hours or overnight. Bake, uncovered, in preheated 350°F oven 30 minutes or until heated through.

Nutrients per Serving (½ of total recipe (without peperoncini)): Calories: 282, Total Fat: 7 g, Calories from Fat: 23%, Saturated Fat: 3 g, Cholesterol: 31 mg, Sodium: 368 mg, Carbohydrate: 37 g, Dietary Fiber: 3 g, Protein: 16 g

Dietary Exchanges: 2 Starch, 2 Vegetable, 1 Lean Meat, 1 Fat

Chunky Beef and Pepper Casserole with Noodles

Prep Time: 15 minutes • **Cook Time:** 15 minutes
Stand Time: 5 minutes

1 pound 95% lean ground beef
1 cup chopped green bell pepper
1 cup chopped yellow onion
1 (8-ounce) can tomato sauce with basil, garlic and oregano
2 teaspoons Worcestershire sauce
4 ounces uncooked no-yolk egg noodles
¼ teaspoon salt
½ cup chopped fresh parsley

1. Heat 12-inch skillet over medium-high heat until hot. Add beef; cook and stir 4 minutes or until no longer pink. Drain. Set aside.

2. Add pepper and onion to skillet; cook and stir 4 minutes or until onion is translucent. Return beef to skillet. Add tomato sauce and Worcestershire sauce; stir to blend. Bring to a boil. Reduce heat. Cover and simmer 15 minutes or until onion is tender.

3. Meanwhile, cook pasta according to package directions, omitting salt and fat.

4. Remove meat mixture from heat; stir in salt. Cover; let stand 5 minutes. Serve beef mixture over cooked pasta. *Makes 4 servings*

Nutrients per Serving (1 cup beef and pepper mixture with ½ cup cooked noodles): Calories: 352, Total Fat: 8 g, Calories from Fat: 22%, Saturated Fat: 2 g, Cholesterol: 66 mg, Sodium: 432 mg, Carbohydrate: 36 g, Dietary Fiber: 4 g, Protein: 31 g

Dietary Exchanges: 2 Starch, 1 Vegetable, 3 Lean Meat

Beef & Bean Burritos

  Nonstick cooking spray
½ pound beef round steak, cut into ½-inch pieces
3 cloves garlic, minced
1 can (about 15 ounces) pinto beans, rinsed and drained
1 can (about 4 ounces) diced mild green chiles, drained
¼ cup finely chopped fresh cilantro
6 (6-inch) flour tortillas, warmed
½ cup (2 ounces) shredded reduced-fat Cheddar cheese
  Salsa (optional)
  Fat-free sour cream (optional)

1. Spray nonstick skillet with cooking spray; heat over medium heat until hot. Add steak and garlic; cook and stir 5 minutes or until steak is cooked to desired doneness.

2. Stir beans, chiles and cilantro into skillet; cook and stir 5 minutes or until heated through.

3. Spoon steak mixture evenly down center of each tortilla; sprinkle cheese evenly over steak mixture. Fold bottom end of tortilla over filling; roll to enclose. Serve with salsa and sour cream, if desired.

Makes 6 servings

Nutrients per Serving (1 burrito (without salsa and sour cream)): Calories: 278, Total Fat: 7 g, Calories from Fat: 22%, Saturated Fat: 2 g, Cholesterol: 31 mg, Sodium: 956 mg, Carbohydrate: 36 g, Dietary Fiber: 1 g, Protein: 19 g

Dietary Exchanges: 2 Starch, 1 Vegetable, 1½ Lean Meat, ½ Fat

Veal in Gingered Sweet Bell Pepper Sauce

1 teaspoon olive oil
¾ pound thinly sliced veal cutlets
½ cup fat-free (skim) milk
1 tablespoon finely chopped fresh tarragon
2 teaspoons crushed capers
1 jar (7 ounces) roasted red peppers, drained
1 tablespoon lemon juice
½ teaspoon grated fresh ginger
½ teaspoon black pepper
   Additional fresh tarragon (optional)

1. Heat oil in medium saucepan over high heat. Add veal; lightly brown both sides. Reduce heat to medium. Add milk, chopped tarragon and capers. Cook, uncovered, 5 minutes or until veal is fork-tender and milk evaporates.

2. Place roasted peppers, lemon juice, ginger and black pepper in food processor or blender; process until smooth. Set aside.

3. Remove veal from pan with slotted spoon, reserving capers. Spoon roasted pepper sauce over veal. Sprinkle with cooked capers and fresh tarragon, if desired. *Makes 4 servings*

Nutrients per Serving (¼ of total recipe): Calories: 120, Total Fat: 4 g, Calories from Fat: 31%, Saturated Fat: 1 g, Cholesterol: 54 mg, Sodium: 89 mg, Carbohydrate: 6 g, Dietary Fiber: 1 g, Protein: 14 g

Dietary Exchanges: 1 Vegetable, 2 Lean Meat

Asparagus with No-Cook
Creamy Mustard Sauce
(p. 88)

Fresh Cranberry-Pineapple
Congeal (p. 90)

Zucchini Cakes (p. 104)

Broccoli Supreme (p. 92)

Slimming Sides

Asparagus with No-Cook Creamy Mustard Sauce

½ cup plain fat-free yogurt
2 tablespoons reduced-fat mayonnaise
1 tablespoon Dijon mustard
2 teaspoons lemon juice
½ teaspoon salt
2 cups water
1½ pounds asparagus spears, rinsed and trimmed
    Black pepper

1. For sauce, combine yogurt, mayonnaise, mustard, lemon juice and salt in small bowl. Whisk until smooth and set aside.

2. Bring water to a boil in 12-inch skillet over high heat. Add asparagus, return to a boil, reduce heat, cover tightly and simmer 3 minutes or until just crisp-tender. Drain on paper towels.

3. Place asparagus on serving platter and spoon sauce over all. Sprinkle with black pepper. *Makes 6 servings*

Nutrients per Serving (about 6 spears with 2 tablespoons sauce): Calories: 57, Total Fat: 2 g, Calories from Fat: 28%, Saturated Fat: <1 g, Cholesterol: 2 mg, Sodium: 299 mg, Carbohydrate: 8 g, Dietary Fiber: 2 g, Protein: 4 g

Dietary Exchanges: 2 Vegetable

Fresh Cranberry-Pineapple Congeal

Prep Time: 10 minutes • **Chill Time:** 1 hour

1 medium orange
1 cup fresh or thawed frozen cranberries
⅔ cup water
1 package (4-serving size) sugar-free raspberry-flavored gelatin
1 cup ice cubes
½ (8-ounce) can crushed pineapple in juice, drained

1. Grate orange peel into small bowl; set aside. Coarsely chop cranberries in blender or food processor; set aside.

2. Squeeze juice from orange into small saucepan. Stir in water; stir to combine. Bring to a boil over high heat. Remove from heat. Stir in gelatin until completely dissolved. Add ice cubes; stir until gelatin is slightly thickened. Remove any unmelted pieces of ice.

3. Stir in cranberries, pineapple and reserved orange peel. Pour mixture into four 6-ounce glass dishes. Cover with plastic wrap; refrigerate until firm.

Makes 4 servings

Nutrients per Serving (½ cup): Calories: 59, Total Fat: <1 g, Calories from Fat: 2%, Saturated Fat: <1 g, Cholesterol: 0 mg, Sodium: 56 mg, Carbohydrate: 13 g, Dietary Fiber: 2 g, Protein: 2 g

Dietary Exchanges: 1 Fruit

Broccoli
Supreme

2 packages (10 ounces) frozen chopped broccoli
1 cup fat-free reduced-sodium chicken broth
2 tablespoons reduced-fat mayonnaise
2 teaspoons instant minced onion (optional)

1. Combine broccoli, chicken broth, mayonnaise and onion, if desired, in large saucepan. Simmer, covered, stirring occasionally, until broccoli is tender.

2. Uncover; continue to simmer, stirring occasionally, until most liquid has evaporated.   *Makes 7 servings*

Nutrients per Serving (about ¾ cup): Calories: 31, Total Fat: 1 g, Calories from Fat: 25%, Saturated Fat: <1 g, Cholesterol: 1 mg, Sodium: 26 mg, Carbohydrate: 4 g, Dietary Fiber: 2 g, Protein: 2 g

Dietary Exchanges: 1 Vegetable

Mashed Squash

1 medium acorn squash, halved and seeded
1 tablespoon maple syrup or maple-flavored syrup
½ teaspoon pumpkin pie spice*
 Butter-flavored salt (optional)
 Black pepper (optional)

Substitute ¼ teaspoon ground cinnamon, ⅛ teaspoon ground ginger and pinch each ground allspice and ground nutmeg for ½ teaspoon pumpkin pie spice.

1. Preheat oven to 400°F. Place squash halves, cut sides down, on baking sheet. Bake 30 minutes or until tender.

2. Scoop squash pulp into large bowl; beat with electric mixer. Stir in syrup and pumpkin pie spice. Season to taste with salt and pepper, if desired. *Makes 4 servings*

Nutrients per Serving (¼ of total recipe (without salt and pepper)): Calories: 70, Total Fat: <1 g, Calories from Fat: 2%, Saturated Fat: <1 g, Cholesterol: 0 mg, Sodium: 5 mg, Carbohydrate: 18 g, Dietary Fiber: 2 g, Protein: 1 g

Dietary Exchanges: 1 Starch

Creamy Dilled Peas

2 cups frozen peas
1 cup thin onion wedges
¼ cup low-fat sour cream
2 tablespoons reduced-fat cream cheese, softened
1 tablespoon fat-free (skim) milk
1 teaspoon all-purpose flour
1 teaspoon chopped fresh dill *or* **¼ teaspoon dried dill weed**
¼ teaspoon grated lemon peel
⅛ teaspoon black pepper

1. Bring 1 cup water to a boil in medium saucepan over high heat. Add peas and onions; return to a boil. Reduce heat to medium-low. Simmer, covered, 4 to 5 minutes or until vegetables are crisp-tender. Drain vegetables; return to saucepan.

2. Combine sour cream, cream cheese, milk, flour, dill, lemon peel and pepper in small bowl. Stir into vegetables in saucepan. Cook and stir over medium heat until mixture boils and thickens. Cook and stir 1 minute more.   *Makes 4 servings*

Nutrients per Serving (¾ cup): Calories: 113, Total Fat: 2 g, Calories from Fat: 20%, Saturated Fat: 1 g, Cholesterol: 7 mg, Sodium: 122 mg, Carbohydrate: 17 g, Dietary Fiber: 4 g, Protein: 6 g

Dietary Exchanges: ½ Milk, 2 Vegetable, ½ Fat

Low-Fat Cajun Wedges

4 medium russet potatoes
Nonstick cooking spray
1 tablespoon Cajun seasoning or other seasoning, such as paprika
Purple kale and fresh sage leaves (optional)

1. Preheat oven to 400°F. Scrub potatoes under running water with soft vegetable brush; rinse. Dry well. (Do not peel.) Line baking sheet with foil and spray with cooking spray.

2. Cut potatoes in half lengthwise; then cut each half lengthwise into 3 wedges. Place potatoes, skin side down, in single layer on prepared baking sheet. Spray potatoes lightly with cooking spray; sprinkle with seasoning.

3. Bake 25 minutes or until browned and fork-tender. Serve immediately.

Makes 4 servings

Low-Fat Potato Chips: Follow step 1 as directed. Slice potatoes crosswise as thin as possible. Place in single layer on prepared baking sheet; spray and season as directed. Bake 10 to 15 minutes or until browned and crisp. Serve immediately.

Low-Fat Cottage Fries: Follow step 1 as directed. Cut potatoes crosswise into 1/4-inch-thick slices. Place in single layer on prepared baking sheet; spray and season as directed. Bake 15 to 20 minutes or until browned and fork-tender. Serve immediately.

Nutrients per Serving (3 wedges): Calories: 127, Total Fat: <1 g, Calories from Fat: 3%, Saturated Fat: <1 g, Cholesterol: 0 mg, Sodium: 153 mg, Carbohydrate: 29 g, Dietary Fiber: 3 g, Protein: 3 g
Dietary Exchanges: 2 Starch

Corn
Casserole

2 cups grated zucchini
1 cup frozen corn
1 cup diced red bell pepper
2 cups cholesterol-free egg substitute
½ cup fat-free evaporated milk
2 teaspoons sugar substitute
¼ teaspoon celery seed
⅛ teaspoon salt
⅛ teaspoon red pepper flakes (optional)

1. Preheat oven to 350°F. Coat 11×7-inch baking dish with nonstick cooking spray.

2. Mix zucchini, corn and bell pepper in baking dish. Whisk egg substitute, evaporated milk, celery seed, salt and red pepper flakes, if desired, in medium bowl; pour over vegetables in baking dish. Bake 45 to 55 minutes or until golden. *Makes 10 servings*

Nutrients per Serving (½ cup): Calories: 54, Total Fat: <1 g, Calories from Fat: <1%, Saturated Fat: 0 g, Cholesterol: <1 mg, Sodium: 138 mg, Carbohydrate: 7 g, Dietary Fiber: 1 g, Protein: 6 g

Dietary Exchanges: 1 Vegetable, 1 Lean Meat

Garlic Green Beans

1 pound green beans, trimmed
2 tablespoons butter
6 cloves garlic, thinly sliced
2 tablespoons Japanese-style bread crumbs*

*Japanese-style bread crumbs, known as panko, are available in the Asian section of most grocery stores. Plain bread crumbs can be substituted; however, plain bread crumbs contain more carbs than panko. Add 5g carbs per serving if using regular bread crumbs.

1. Fill large bowl with ice and water; set aside. Place beans in large saucepan; cover with water. Bring to a boil; boil 3 minutes or until crisp-tender. Drain beans in colander and immediately plunge into ice water to stop cooking. Drain and pat dry.

2. Heat butter in medium nonstick skillet over medium-high heat. Add garlic; cook and stir until golden. Add beans; cook and stir 2 minutes. Sprinkle bread crumbs over beans; cook and stir 1 to 2 minutes or until bread crumbs are lightly browned. *Makes 4 servings*

Nutrients per Serving (½ cup): Calories: 103, Total Fat: 6 g, Calories from Fat: 51%, Saturated Fat: 4 g, Cholesterol: 16 mg, Sodium: 74 mg, Carbohydrate: 11 g, Dietary Fiber: 4 g, Protein: 3 g

Dietary Exchanges: 2 Vegetable, 1 Fat

Health Nut Brown Rice

½ cup shredded carrot
½ cup shredded zucchini
3 tablespoons sunflower kernels
3 tablespoons sliced almonds
¼ teaspoon red pepper flakes (optional)
1 teaspoon margarine
3 cups cooked brown rice (cooked in chicken broth)
2 tablespoons snipped parsley

Cook carrot, zucchini, sunflower kernels, almonds and pepper flakes in margarine in large skillet over medium-high heat until almonds are browned. Add rice and parsley; stir until heated. *Makes 6 servings*

To microwave: Combine carrot, zucchini, sunflower kernels, almonds, pepper flakes and margarine in 2-quart microproof-baking dish. Cook on HIGH 3 to 4 minutes or until almonds are lightly browned. Add rice and parsley; cook on HIGH 3 to 4 minutes, stirring after 2 minutes, or until heated.

Favorite recipe from **USA Rice**

Nutrients per Serving (⅙ of total recipe): Calories: 182, Total Fat: 6 g, Calories from Fat: 31%, Saturated Fat: 1 g, Cholesterol: 0 mg, Sodium: 347 mg, Carbohydrate: 27 g, Dietary Fiber: 2 g, Protein: 5 g

Dietary Exchanges: 2 Starch, 1 Fat

Sweet-Sour Cabbage with Apples and Caraway Seeds

4 cups shredded red cabbage
1 large tart apple, peeled, quartered, cut crosswise into
   ¼-inch-thick slices
¼ cup *each* packed light brown sugar and cider vinegar
¼ cup water
½ teaspoon salt
¼ teaspoon caraway seeds
   Dash black pepper

1. Combine all ingredients in large saucepan. Cook, covered, over medium heat 10 minutes.

2. Stir mixture. Cook, covered, over medium-low heat 15 to 20 minutes or until cabbage and apple are tender. Serve warm or chilled.

Makes 6 servings

Nutrients per Serving (⅙ of total recipe): Calories: 62, Total Fat: <1 g, Calories from Fat: 2%, Saturated Fat: <1 g, Cholesterol: 0 mg, Sodium: 191 mg, Carbohydrate: 16 g, Dietary Fiber: 2 g, Protein: 1 g

Dietary Exchanges: ½ Fruit, 1 Vegetable

Zucchini Cakes

2 cups grated zucchini
¼ cup *each* **chopped green onions and chopped fresh parsley**
¼ cup all-purpose flour
1 egg
¼ teaspoon garlic salt
 Nonstick cooking spray
 Low-fat sour cream and lemon wedges (optional)

1. Combine all ingredients except cooking spray, sour cream and lemon wedges in bowl of food processor or blender. Process until well combined. Pour batter into medium bowl; set aside.

2. Heat small skillet over low heat for 1 minute; lightly spray with cooking spray. Spoon 2 tablespoons batter into skillet; cook 1 to 2 minutes on each side. Serve with sour cream and lemon wedges.

Makes 8 servings

Nutrients per Serving (1 cake): Calories: 29, Total Fat: <1 g, Calories from Fat: 22%, Saturated Fat: <1 g, Cholesterol: 27 mg, Sodium: 40 mg, Carbohydrate: 4 g, Dietary Fiber: <1 g, Protein: 2 g

Dietary Exchanges: ½ Starch

Chicken with Piquant
Raspberry Sauce (p. 108)

Spicy Mesquite Chicken
Fettuccine (p. 110)

Mediterranean Chicken Couscous (p. 124)

Cajun Chicken Drums (p. 118)

Chicken & Turkey

Chicken with Piquant Raspberry Sauce

4 boneless skinless chicken breasts (about 6 ounces each)*
½ teaspoon salt
¼ teaspoon black pepper
1½ teaspoons *each* unsalted butter and olive oil
½ cup reduced-sodium chicken broth
2 tablespoons balsamic vinegar
2 teaspoons prepared mustard
¼ cup seedless raspberry jam

If chicken cutlets are available, substitute 8 cutlets (about 1½ pounds).

1. Season chicken with salt and pepper. Heat butter and olive oil in large nonstick skillet over medium-high heat.

2. Add chicken; cook 10 to 12 minutes, turning once, until chicken is no longer pink in center.

3. Blend chicken broth, vinegar and mustard; add to pan. Simmer over medium-high heat until sauce is reduced by half. Add raspberry jam, and continue cooking until jam has melted and sauce cooks down to ⅓ cup. Serve sauce with chicken.   *Makes 4 servings*

Nutrients per Serving (1 chicken breast with 4 teaspoons of sauce):
Calories: 216, Total Fat: 5 g, Calories from Fat: 21%, Saturated Fat: 2 g, Cholesterol: 71 mg, Sodium: 432 mg, Carbohydrate: 15 g, Dietary Fiber: <1 g, Protein: 26 g

Dietary Exchanges: 1 Starch, 3 Lean Meat

Spicy Mesquite Chicken Fettuccine

8 ounces uncooked fettuccine
1 tablespoon chili powder
1 teaspoon *each* **ground cumin and paprika**
¼ teaspoon ground red pepper
2 teaspoons vegetable oil
1 pound mesquite marinated chicken breasts, cut into bite-size pieces

1. Cook pasta according to package directions, omitting salt. Drain; set aside.

2. Meanwhile, combine chili powder, cumin, paprika and red pepper in small bowl; set aside.

3. Heat oil in large nonstick skillet over medium-high heat until hot. Add chili powder mixture; cook 30 seconds, stirring constantly. Add chicken; cook and stir 5 to 6 minutes or until cooked through and lightly browned. Add pasta to skillet; stir. Cook 1 to 2 minutes or until heated through. Sprinkle with additional chili powder, if desired.   *Makes 4 servings*

Nutrients per Serving (¼ of total recipe): Calories: 520, Total Fat: 8 g, Calories from Fat: 14%, Saturated Fat: 2 g, Cholesterol: 144 mg, Sodium: 699 mg, Carbohydrate: 71 g, Dietary Fiber: 2 g, Protein: 44 g

Dietary Exchanges: 4 Starch, 4 Lean Meat

Taco Pizza

Prep Time: 15 minutes • **Bake Time:** 7 to 8 minutes

1 package (10 ounces) refrigerated pizza dough
¾ pound 93% lean ground turkey
½ cup chopped onion
1 can (8 ounces) tomato sauce
1 envelope (1.25 ounces) reduced-sodium taco seasoning
2 medium plum tomatoes, thinly sliced, *or* 1 cup chopped tomato
1 cup (4 ounces) shredded reduced-fat Cheddar cheese
1½ cups shredded lettuce

1. Preheat oven to 425°F. Lightly spray 12-inch pizza pan with nonstick cooking spray. Unroll pizza dough; press into prepared pan. Build up edges slightly. Prick dough with fork. Bake 7 to 10 minutes or until lightly browned.

2. Meanwhile, lightly spray large nonstick skillet with cooking spray. Add turkey and onion; cook and stir until turkey is no longer pink. Add tomato sauce and taco seasoning to skillet. Bring to a boil. Reduce heat; simmer, uncovered, 2 to 3 minutes. Spoon turkey mixture on top of warm pizza crust. Bake 5 minutes.

3. Arrange tomatoes on top of turkey mixture. Sprinkle with cheese. Bake 2 to 3 minutes more or until cheese melts. Top with lettuce. Cut into 8 pieces before serving.   *Makes 4 servings*

Nutrients per Serving (2 slices): Calories: 422, Total Fat: 10 g, Calories from Fat: 21%, Saturated Fat: 2 g, Cholesterol: 54 mg, Sodium: 740 mg, Carbohydrate: 48 g, Dietary Fiber: 3 g, Protein: 34 g

Dietary Exchanges: 3 Starch, 1 Vegetable, 3 Lean Meat

Chicken
Santiago

4 skinless boneless chicken breast halves
Pepper
½ **cup low sodium chicken bouillon or water**
1 **tablespoon cornstarch**
⅓ **cup apple juice**
2 **cups Chilean seedless red or green grapes, halved**
¼ **cup half-and-half**
1 **green onion, thinly sliced**
¼ **teaspoon dried thyme leaves**
⅛ **teaspoon ground ginger**

Oven Directions
Preheat oven to 375°F. Season chicken with pepper; place in baking dish. Add bouillon to dish. Cover with aluminum foil. Bake 20 to 30 minutes or until firm and opaque. Pour ½ cup juices from chicken into saucepan. Add cornstarch mixed with apple juice; stir to blend well. Stir in remaining ingredients. Cook and stir over medium-high heat until sauce bubbles and thickens, about 3 minutes. Season to taste with pepper. Serve sauce over chicken. *Makes 4 servings*

Microwave Directions: Season chicken with pepper; place in round microwavable dish with thickest ends toward outside of dish. Add bouillon to dish. Cover with waxed paper. Microwave on HIGH (100% power) 6 to 8 minutes or until firm and opaque, turning and rearranging chicken after 4 minutes. Pour ½ cup juices from chicken into microwavable bowl; cover chicken and set aside. Stir cornstarch into apple juice; add to reserved chicken juices along with remaining ingredients. Microwave on HIGH 4 to 5 minutes until sauce bubbles and thickens, stirring twice during cooking. Season to taste with pepper. Serve sauce over chicken.

Favorite recipe from **Chilean Fresh Fruit Association**

Nutrients per Serving (¼ of total recipe): Calories: 221, Total Fat: 3 g, Calories from Fat: 13%, Saturated Fat: 1 g, Cholesterol: 74 mg, Sodium: 159 mg, Carbohydrate: 20 g, Dietary Fiber: 1 g, Protein: 28 g
Dietary Exchanges: 1 Fruit, 3½ Lean Meat

Peppered Turkey Medallions with Chutney Sauce

1 tablespoon mixed peppercorns
1 pound turkey tenderloins, cut into ¾-inch medallions
1 teaspoon margarine
2 teaspoons olive oil, divided
2 tablespoons finely chopped green onion
¼ cup turkey broth or reduced sodium chicken broth
2 tablespoons brandy
¼ cup prepared chutney

Crush peppercorns in spice grinder, food processor or mortar with pestle. Press peppercorns onto both sides of turkey medallions. Refrigerate 30 minutes.

Heat margarine and 1 teaspoon oil over medium heat in large nonstick skillet. Add medallions; cook and stir 5 minutes per side or until no longer pink in center. Remove medallions from pan and keep warm.

Add remaining 1 teaspoon oil to skillet; add onion. Cook and stir 30 seconds. Add broth and cook 45 seconds to reduce liquid. Stir in brandy and cook 1 to 2 minutes. Reduce heat to low; blend in chutney.

To serve, pour chutney sauce over medallions.   *Makes 4 servings*

Favorite recipe from **National Turkey Federation**

Nutrients per Serving (¼ of total recipe): Calories: 218, Total Fat: 4 g, Calories from Fat: 16%, Saturated Fat: 1 g, Cholesterol: 70 mg, Sodium: 142 mg, Carbohydrate: 11 g, Dietary Fiber: 1 g, Protein: 28 g
Dietary Exchanges: ½ Fruit, 4 Lean Meat

Broiled Chicken Salad

4 boneless skinless chicken breasts (about 1 pound)
1 can (15 ounces) black beans, rinsed and drained
2 green onions, chopped
1 tablespoon plus 8 teaspoons reduced-fat oil and vinegar dressing, divided
1 package (10 ounces) frozen corn, thawed and drained
2 tablespoons chopped pimiento
2 tablespoons chopped fresh cilantro
2 large tomatoes, cut into wedges

1. Preheat broiler. Position oven rack about 4 inches from heat source.

2. Place chicken on rack of broiler pan. Broil 8 minutes or until browned on both sides and no longer pink in center, turning after 4 minutes. Set aside.

3. Meanwhile, combine beans, onions and 1 tablespoon dressing in medium bowl; mix lightly. Set aside. Combine corn, pimiento and chopped cilantro in separate bowl; mix lightly. Set aside.

4. Diagonally cut each chicken piece into thick slices; arrange on salad plates. Arrange tomato wedges and spoonfuls of bean and corn mixtures around chicken. Drizzle 2 teaspoons dressing over each piece of chicken. Serve with additional dressing, if desired.   *Makes 4 servings*

Nutrients per Serving (¼ of total recipe): Calories: 310, Total Fat: 4 g, Calories from Fat: 11%, Saturated Fat: 1 g, Cholesterol: 66 mg, Sodium: 344 mg, Carbohydrate: 36 g, Dietary Fiber: 7 g, Protein: 34 g

Dietary Exchanges: 2 Starch, 1 Vegetable, 3½ Lean Meat

Cajun Chicken Drums

4 chicken drumsticks, skin removed
½ to ¾ teaspoon Cajun seasoning
½ teaspoon grated lemon peel
2 tablespoons lemon juice
½ teaspoon hot pepper sauce
⅛ teaspoon salt
2 tablespoons finely chopped fresh parsley

1. Preheat oven to 400°F. Coat shallow baking dish with nonstick cooking spray. Arrange chicken in dish and sprinkle evenly with Cajun seasoning. Cover dish with foil and bake 25 minutes, turning drumsticks once.

2. Remove foil and cook 15 to 20 minutes longer or until chicken is no longer pink in center. Remove from oven; add remaining ingredients and toss to blend, scraping bottom and sides of baking dish with spatula.

Makes 2 servings

Nutrients per Serving (2 drumsticks): Calories: 173, Total Fat: 5 g, Calories from Fat: 25%, Saturated Fat: 1 g, Cholesterol: 108 mg, Sodium: 254 mg, Carbohydrate: 2 g, Dietary Fiber: <1 g, Protein: 29 g

Dietary Exchanges: 3 Lean Meat

Fettuccine with Turkey Bolognese Sauce

1 teaspoon olive oil
2 carrots, chopped
1 small onion, chopped
1 rib celery, chopped
1 to 1½ pounds lean ground turkey
¼ cup dry red wine or chicken broth
1 jar (1 pound 10 ounces) RAGÚ® Light Pasta Sauce
2 tablespoons chopped fresh parsley
1 box (16 ounces) fettuccine, cooked and drained

In 12-inch nonstick skillet, heat olive oil over medium heat and cook carrots, onion and celery, stirring frequently, 5 minutes or until tender. Add turkey and cook, breaking up with spoon, until turkey is thoroughly cooked. Stir in wine. Bring to a boil over high heat. Reduce heat to low and simmer uncovered 3 minutes. Stir in Ragú Light Pasta Sauce and parsley; simmer, stirring occasionally, 5 minutes. Season, if desired, with salt and ground black pepper. Serve over hot fettuccine.

Makes 6 servings

Nutrients per Serving (1/6 of total recipe): Calories: 424, Total Fat: 11 g, Calories from Fat: 23%, Saturated Fat: 2 g, Cholesterol: 69 mg, Sodium: 490 mg, Carbohydrate: 55 g, Dietary Fiber: 3 g, Protein: 26 g

Dietary Exchanges: 3 Starch, 2 Vegetable, 2 Lean Meat, 1 Fat

Shrimp and Chicken Paella

¾ cup ready-to-serve rice
2 cans (about 14 ounces each) low-sodium diced tomatoes
½ teaspoon ground turmeric *or* 1 teaspoon saffron threads
1 package (12 ounces) frozen shrimp, thawed, peeled and deveined (about 3 cups)
2 chicken tenders (about 4 ounces), cut into bite-size pieces
1 cup frozen peas, thawed

1. Preheat oven to 400°F. Lightly coat 8-inch square glass baking dish with nonstick cooking spray. Place rice in baking dish, shaking to distribute evenly.

2. Empty 1 can of tomatoes with juice over rice; sprinkle turmeric over tomatoes. Arrange shrimp and chicken over tomatoes. Top with peas.

3. Drain second can of tomatoes; discard juice. Arrange tomatoes evenly over shrimp and chicken. Cover casserole with 9-inch square of waxed paper. Bake 30 minutes. Remove from oven and let stand, covered, 5 minutes.

Makes 6 servings

Serving Suggestion: Serve with a green salad tossed with mustard vinaigrette and garnished with ½ cup drained, no-salt-added canned corn kernels.

Nutrients per Serving (1 cup): Calories: 175, Total Fat: 1 g, Calories from Fat: 7%, Saturated Fat: <1 g, Cholesterol: 97 mg, Sodium: 152 mg, Carbohydrate: 19 g, Dietary Fiber: 2 g, Protein: 19 g

Dietary Exchanges: 1 Starch, 1 Vegetable, 2 Lean Meat

Curried Chicken Cutlets

4 boneless skinless chicken breasts (about 1 pound)
½ cup all-purpose flour
1 teaspoon salt
1 teaspoon ground red pepper
1 tablespoon curry powder
2 red bell peppers, cut lengthwise into ¼-inch-thick slices
1 teaspoon olive oil
¼ cup lemon juice
¼ cup finely chopped fresh cilantro
   Kale (optional)
   Fresh marjoram (optional)

1. Pound chicken breasts to ¼-inch thickness between 2 pieces of plastic wrap with flat side of meat mallet or rolling pin.

2. Combine flour, salt, ground red pepper and curry powder in shallow bowl. Dip chicken cutlets in flour mixture to coat both sides well; shake off excess flour.

3. Generously spray nonstick skillet with nonstick cooking spray; heat over medium heat. Add 2 chicken cutlets; cook 3 to 4 minutes per side. Transfer to warm plate; cover and set aside. Repeat with remaining chicken.

4. Add bell peppers and olive oil to skillet; cook and stir 5 minutes or until peppers are tender. Stir in lemon juice and cilantro; heat through. Pour sauce over chicken cutlets. Garnish with kale and fresh marjoram, if desired. *Makes 4 servings*

Nutrients per Serving (1 cutlet with about ½ cup sauce): Calories: 230, Total Fat: 5 g, Calories from Fat: 18%, Saturated Fat: 1 g, Cholesterol: 73 mg, Sodium: 599 mg, Carbohydrate: 17 g, Dietary Fiber: 1 g, Protein: 29 g

Dietary Exchanges: 1 Starch, 3 Lean Meat

Mediterranean Chicken Couscous

Prep Time: 15 minutes • **Cook Time:** 15 minutes

2⅓ cups fat-free reduced-sodium chicken broth, divided
½ cup dry white wine
3 teaspoons minced garlic, divided
1 teaspoon fennel seeds
12 ounces boneless skinless chicken breasts, cut into 4 pieces
1⅓ cups quick-cooking couscous
¼ cup finely chopped Italian parsley
1 cup canned chickpeas, rinsed and drained
⅔ cup chopped tomato
2 tablespoons snipped chives

1. Combine 1 cup chicken broth, wine, 2 teaspoons garlic and fennel in large skillet. Heat over medium-high heat 2 to 3 minutes; add chicken. Reduce heat to low; simmer, covered, 1 minute. Turn chicken; simmer, covered, 3 to 4 additional minutes.

2. Meanwhile, place remaining 1⅓ cups chicken broth in medium saucepan. Bring to a boil over high heat. Stir in couscous; cover. Remove saucepan from heat; let stand 5 minutes. Stir in remaining 1 teaspoon garlic and parsley.

3. Add chickpeas and tomatoes to chicken mixture. Simmer, covered, 2 additional minutes.

4. Spoon couscous into each serving bowl; top with chicken breast and broth mixture. Top with 1½ teaspoons chives.   *Makes 4 servings*

Nutrients per Serving (1 cup (¾ cup couscous, 1 piece of chicken and ½ cup broth mixture)): Calories: 437, Total Fat: 4 g, Calories from Fat: 9%, Saturated Fat: 1 g, Cholesterol: 52 mg, Sodium: 267 mg, Carbohydrate: 62 g, Dietary Fiber: 12 g, Protein: 31 g

Dietary Exchanges: 4 Starch, 1 Vegetable, 2½ Lean Meat

Asparagus and Chicken Stir-Fry

2 teaspoons olive oil
1 cup onion slices
1 clove garlic, minced
½ pound boneless skinless chicken breast, cut into 2-inch pieces
1½ pounds asparagus,* trimmed and diagonally sliced into 2-inch pieces
2 cups red bell pepper cubes
1 tablespoon chopped fresh basil *or* **1 teaspoon dried basil**
½ teaspoon salt
⅛ teaspoon black pepper

*You may substitute two 8-ounce packages frozen asparagus for the fresh asparagus. Partially thaw before using.

1. Heat oil in large nonstick skillet or wok. Add onion and garlic; stir-fry over medium-high heat 1 minute or until onion is softened. Add chicken; stir-fry 3 minutes or until chicken is no longer pink.

2. Add asparagus, bell pepper, basil, salt and black pepper; stir-fry 3 to 4 minutes or until asparagus is crisp-tender.   *Makes 4 servings*

Note: This dish can be served with hot rice or pasta.

Nutrients per Serving (¼ of total recipe): Calories: 143, Total Fat: 5 g, Calories from Fat: 29%, Saturated Fat: <1 g, Cholesterol: 29 mg, Sodium: 316 mg, Carbohydrate: 9 g, Dietary Fiber: 3 g, Protein: 16 g
Dietary Exchanges: 2 Vegetable, 1½ Lean Meat

Grilled Chicken with Extra Spicy Corn and Black Beans

Preparation Time: 10 minutes • Cook Time: 12 minutes

3 tablespoons MRS. DASH® Extra Spicy Seasoning Blend, divided
1 cup canned black beans, drained and rinsed
1 cup frozen yellow corn, thawed, cooked and cooled
1 medium red bell pepper, seeded and chopped (optional)
¼ cup finely chopped red onion
½ cup finely chopped fresh cilantro
2 tablespoons fresh lime juice
4 boneless skinless chicken breast halves

At least one hour before grilling chicken, to prepare Salsa, mix 2 tablespoons Mrs. Dash® Extra Spicy Seasoning, black beans, yellow corn, pepper (if using), red onion, cilantro and fresh lime juice until well blended. Set aside, stirring once or twice. To prepare Chicken, preheat grill to medium high. Place 1 tablespoon Mrs. Dash® Extra Spicy in plastic bag. Place chicken in bag and shake until well coated. Place on grill and cook 5 minutes. Turn and cook additional 5 minutes, or until juices run clear when skewer is inserted. Serve hot with salsa on the side.

Makes 4 servings

Nutrients per Serving (¼ of total recipe): Calories: 220, Total Fat: 2 g, Calories from Fat: 7%, Saturated Fat: <1 g, Cholesterol: 66 mg, Sodium: 262 mg, Carbohydrate: 20 g, Dietary Fiber: 4 g, Protein: 31 g

Dietary Exchanges: 1 Starch, 1 Vegetable, 2½ Lean Meat

Mint Chocolate Cups
(p. 136)

Minted Pear with
Gorgonzola (p. 146)

Cinnamon Dessert Taco
with Fruit Salsa (p. 142)

Blueberry-Pear Tart
(p. 130)

Satisfying Desserts

Blueberry-Pear Tart

Prep Time: 10 minutes • **Bake Time:** 12 minutes • **Chill Time:** 2 hours

1 refrigerated pie crust
1 medium fully ripened pear, peeled, cored and thinly sliced
8 ounces fresh or thawed frozen blueberries or blackberries
⅓ cup no-sugar-added raspberry fruit spread
½ teaspoon grated fresh ginger

1. Preheat oven to 450°F.

2. Spray 9-inch tart pan with nonstick cooking spray. Place dough in pan; press against side of pan to form ½-inch edge. Prick dough with fork. Bake 12 minutes. Remove pan to wire rack; cool completely.

3. Arrange pears on bottom of cooled crust; top with blueberries.

4. Place fruit spread in small microwavable bowl. Cover with plastic wrap; microwave on HIGH 15 seconds; stir. If necessary, microwave additional 10 to 15 seconds or until spread is melted; stir. Add ginger; stir until blended. Let stand 30 seconds to thicken slightly. Pour mixture over fruit in crust. Refrigerate 2 hours. (Do not cover.) Cut into 8 slices before serving.   *Makes 8 servings*

Nutrients per Serving (1 slice (⅛ of total recipe)): Calories: 179, Total Fat: 7 g, Calories from Fat: 36%, Saturated Fat: 3 g, Cholesterol: 5 mg, Sodium: 101 mg, Carbohydrate: 28 g, Dietary Fiber: 2 g, Protein: 1 g

Dietary Exchanges: 1 Starch, 1 Fruit, 1 Fat

Creamy Rich Fudge

1½ cups EQUAL® Sugar Lite™
⅔ cup evaporated 2% milk
2 tablespoons butter
¼ teaspoon salt
2 cups miniature marshmallows
1½ cups semisweet chocolate chips
1 teaspoon vanilla extract

Combine EQUAL® Sugar Lite™, evaporated milk, butter and salt in medium-sized heavy saucepan. Bring to a rolling boil over medium heat, stirring frequently. Boil and stir 5 minutes. Remove from heat. Line an 8×8×2-inch pan with foil, with 1-inch foil hanging ever edges.

Mix marshmallows, chocolate chips and vanilla with warm milk mixture; stir until completely melted and smooth. Pour mixture into prepared pan. Chill at least 2 hours or until firm to the touch. Lift fudge out of pan with foil; remove foil and cut into squares. Chill fudge until ready to serve. Keep tightly covered in refrigerator for up to 1 week.   *Makes 48 pieces*

Nutrients per Serving (2 pieces): Calories: 106, Total Fat: 4 g, Calories from Fat: 34%, Saturated Fat: 3 g, Cholesterol: 3 mg, Sodium: 37 mg, Carbohydrate: 18 g, Dietary Fiber: 1 g, Protein: 1 g

Dietary Exchanges: 1 Starch, ½ Fat

Lattice-Topped Deep Dish Cherry Pie

Prep Time: 15 minutes • **Bake Time:** 40 to 50 minutes

2 cans (14½ ounces each) pitted red tart cherries in water
½ cup granular sucralose-based sugar substitute
3 tablespoons quick-cooking tapioca
¼ teaspoon almond extract
¾ cup all-purpose flour
¼ teaspoon salt
3 tablespoons shortening
2 to 3 tablespoons cold water

1. Preheat oven to 375°F. Drain 1 can of cherries. Combine drained cherries, can of cherries with juice, sugar substitute, tapioca and almond extract in large bowl. Set aside.

2. Meanwhile, combine flour and salt in small bowl. Cut in shortening until mixture resembles fine crumbs. Add water, 1 tablespoon at a time, stirring just until dough is moistened; form into ball. Roll dough into 9×8-inch rectangle on lightly floured surface. Cut into nine 8×1-inch strips.

3. Spoon cherry mixture into 13×9-inch baking dish. Place 4 pastry strips horizontally over cherry mixture. Weave remaining 5 pastry strips vertically across horizontal strips. Pinch strips at ends to seal. Bake 40 to 50 minutes or until fruit is bubbly and pastry is light brown. Remove to wire rack; cool slightly. To serve, spoon into bowls. *Makes 9 servings*

Nutrients per Serving (⅔ cup): Calories: 126, Total Fat: 4 g, Calories from Fat: 29%, Saturated Fat: 1 g, Cholesterol: 0 mg, Sodium: 72 mg, Carbohydrate: 21 g, Dietary Fiber: 1 g, Protein: 2 g

Dietary Exchanges: ½ Starch, 1 Fruit, 1 Fat

Mint Chocolate Cups

**2 packages (3 ounces total) sugar-free chocolate
  pudding mix**
2½ cups fat-free half-and-half
½ cup fat-free sour cream
½ to 1 teaspoon peppermint extract
1 teaspoon vanilla extract
1½ cups fat-free whipped topping
6 sugar-free peppermint patties, chopped

1. Whisk pudding mix and half-and-half in medium bowl. Blend sour cream, peppermint and vanilla extracts into prepared pudding until smooth.

2. Divide mixture evenly into 6 parfait glasses or dessert cups, with 2 tablespoons whipped topping in between to make layers. Top each cup with additional 2 tablespoons whipped topping. Chill 1 hour or until completely cool. Garnish each serving with 1 chopped peppermint patty. *Makes 6 servings*

Nutrients per Serving (⅔ cup chocolate mixture with ¼ cup whipped topping): Calories: 166, Total Fat: <1 g, Calories from Fat: <1%, Saturated Fat: 0 g, Cholesterol: 15 mg, Sodium: 541 mg, Carbohydrate: 29 g, Dietary Fiber: <1 g, Protein: 6 g

Dietary Exchanges: 2 Starch

Enlightened Banana Upside-Down Cake

½ **cup sugar**
1 **tablespoon water**
2 **tablespoons butter**
2 **small bananas, sliced ¼ inch thick**
1½ **cups all-purpose flour**
2 **teaspoons baking powder**
½ **teaspoon salt**
¾ **cup sugar substitute***
¼ **cup *each* canola oil and unsweetened applesauce**
3 **egg whites**
1 **egg yolk**
½ **cup low-fat buttermilk**
1 **teaspoon vanilla**

This recipe was tested with sucralose-based sugar substitute.

1. Preheat oven to 325°F.

2. Combine sugar and water in small saucepan. Heat mixture over medium-high heat, stirring mixture and swirling pan, until sugar is amber in color. Stir in butter. Pour mixture immediately into 8-inch square nonstick baking pan. Arrange banana slices in caramel on bottom of pan.

3. Sift flour, baking powder and salt in medium bowl; set aside. Beat sugar substitute, oil and applesauce in large bowl with electric mixer on medium speed 1 minute. Beat in egg whites and yolk, one at a time, until blended Add buttermilk and vanilla. Gradually add flour mixture, beating 1 minute or until blended.

4. Pour batter over bananas in pan. Bake 30 to 35 minutes or until toothpick inserted into center comes out clean. Cool 5 minutes in pan on wire rack; invert onto serving plate. Cool slightly; cut into 12 pieces. Serve warm or at room temperature. *Makes 12 servings*

Nutrients per Serving (2½×2-inch piece of cake): Calories: 184, Total Fat: 7 g, Calories from Fat: 35%, Saturated Fat: 2 g, Cholesterol: 23 mg, Sodium: 191 mg, Carbohydrate: 27 g, Dietary Fiber: 1 g, Protein: 3 g

Dietary Exchanges: 1½ Starch, ½ Fruit, 1 Fat

Nutty Cheesecake Bites

Prep Time: 20 Minutes • **Chill Time:** 45 Minutes

1 package (8 ounces) cream cheese, softened
½ cup SKIPPY® CARB OPTIONS™ Creamy Peanut Spread
¼ cup SPLENDA® No Calorie Sweetener
¼ teaspoon ground cinnamon
¼ teaspoon vanilla extract
Finely chopped peanuts or unsweetened shredded coconut

1. In medium bowl, with electric mixer on medium speed, combine all ingredients except peanuts, scraping down sides of bowl as needed. Chill 30 minutes or until firm.

2. Roll into ¾-inch balls, then roll in peanuts. Chill an additional 15 minutes before serving. *Makes 30 (¾-inch) servings*

Nutrients per Serving (1 cheesecake bite): Calories: 70, Total Fat: 6 g, Calories from Fat: 77%, Saturated Fat: 3 g, Cholesterol: 10 mg, Sodium: 40 mg, Carbohydrate: 2 g, Dietary Fiber: 1 g, Protein: 2 g

Dietary Exchanges: 1½ Fat

Sweet 'n' Easy Fruit Crisp Bowls

2 tablespoons low-fat granola with almonds
1 red apple (8 ounces), such as Gala, diced into ½-inch pieces
1 tablespoon dried sweetened cranberries
¼ teaspoon apple pie spice or ground cinnamon
1 teaspoon margarine
1 packet sugar substitute
¼ teaspoon almond extract
2 tablespoons low-fat vanilla ice cream

1. Place granola in small food storage bag; crush lightly to form coarse crumbs. Set aside.

2. Heat 10-inch nonstick skillet over medium heat until hot. Coat skillet with cooking spray. Add apples, cranberries and apple pie spice. Cook 4 minutes or until apples are just tender, stirring frequently. Remove from heat, stir in margarine, sugar substitute and almond extract. Spoon onto 2 dessert plates. Sprinkle with granola and spoon ice cream on top. Serve immediately.   *Makes 2 servings*

Note: You may prepare apple mixture up to 8 hours in advance. Top with granola and ice cream at time of serving. For a warmed crisp, place apple mixture (before adding granola and ice cream) in microwave and cook 20 to 30 seconds or until slightly heated.

Nutrients per Serving (½ cup apple mixture plus 1 tablespoon granola and 1 tablespoon ice cream): Calories: 150, Total Fat: 3 g, Calories from Fat: 15%, Saturated Fat: <1 g, Cholesterol: <1 mg, Sodium: 40 mg, Carbohydrate: 32 g, Dietary Fiber: 4 g, Protein: 1 g

Dietary Exchanges: 2 Fruit, ½ Fat

Cinnamon Dessert Tacos with Fruit Salsa

1 cup sliced fresh strawberries
1 cup cubed fresh pineapple
1 cup cubed peeled kiwifruit
½ teaspoon minced jalapeño pepper* (optional)
2 packets sugar substitute *or* equivalent of 4 teaspoons sugar (optional)
3 tablespoons sugar
1 tablespoon ground cinnamon
6 (8-inch) flour tortillas
Nonstick cooking spray

*Jalapeño peppers can sting and irritate the skin, so wear rubber gloves when handling peppers and do not touch your eyes.

1. Stir together strawberries, pineapple, kiwifruit, jalapeño pepper and sugar substitute in large bowl; set aside. Combine sugar and cinnamon in small bowl; set aside.

2. Spray tortilla lightly on both sides with cooking spray. Heat over medium heat in nonstick skillet until slightly puffed and golden brown. Remove from heat; immediately dust both sides with cinnamon-sugar mixture. Shake excess cinnamon-sugar back into small bowl. Repeat cooking and dusting process until all tortillas are warmed.

3. Fill tortillas with fruit mixture; fold in half. Serve immediately.

Makes 6 servings

Nutrients per Serving (1 taco with ⅙ of fruit salsa): Calories: 183, Total Fat: 3 g, Calories from Fat: 14%, Saturated Fat: <1 g, Cholesterol: 0 mg, Sodium: 169 mg, Carbohydrate: 36 g, Dietary Fiber: 4 g, Protein: 4 g

Dietary Exchanges: 1½ Starch, 1 Fruit, ½ Fat

Frozen Sundae Pie

26 chocolate wafer cookies
4 cups fat-free ice cream, slightly softened
2 tablespoons fat-free hot fudge topping
1 cup banana slices
2 tablespoons fat-free caramel ice cream topping
1 ounce reduced-fat dry roasted peanuts, crushed

1. Place cookies on bottom and around side of 9-inch pie pan. Carefully spoon ice cream into pie pan; cover with plastic wrap. Freeze 2 hours or overnight until firm.

2. Just before serving, place hot fudge topping in small microwavable bowl; microwave on HIGH 10 seconds. Drizzle pie with fudge topping; top with banana slices. Place caramel topping in small microwavable bowl; microwave on HIGH 10 seconds. Drizzle over bananas; sprinkle with peanuts. *Makes 8 servings*

Note: If desired, this pie can be assembled the night before without the bananas. Top with bananas just before serving.

Nutrients per Serving (1 slice (⅛ of total recipe)): Calories: 252, Total Fat: 5 g, Calories from Fat: 17%, Saturated Fat: 1 g, Cholesterol: <1 mg, Sodium: 210 mg, Carbohydrate: 49 g, Dietary Fiber: 1 g, Protein: 7 g
Dietary Exchanges: 3 Starch, 1 Fat

Minted Pears with Gorgonzola

4 whole firm pears with stems, peeled
2 cups Concord grape juice
1 tablespoon honey
1 tablespoon finely chopped fresh mint
1 cinnamon stick
¼ teaspoon ground nutmeg
¼ cup Gorgonzola cheese, crumbled

1. Place pears in medium saucepan. Add grape juice, honey, mint, cinnamon stick and nutmeg. Bring to a boil over high heat. Cover and simmer 15 to 20 minutes, turning pears once to absorb juices evenly. Cook until pears can be easily pierced with fork. Remove from heat; cool. Remove pears with slotted spoon; set aside. Discard cinnamon stick.

2. Bring juice mixture to a boil; simmer 20 minutes. Pour over pears. Sprinkle Gorgonzola evenly around pears.   *Makes 4 servings*

Nutrients per Serving (1 pear with 1 tablespoon Gorgonzola): Calories: 194, Total Fat: 3 g, Calories from Fat: 13%, Saturated Fat: 2 g, Cholesterol: 6 mg, Sodium: 119 mg, Carbohydrate: 42 g, Dietary Fiber: 4 g, Protein: 2 g

Dietary Exchanges: 2½ Fruit, 1 Fat

Blackberry Strudel Cups

6 sheets frozen phyllo dough, thawed
Nonstick cooking spray
1 pint blackberries
2 tablespoons sugar
1 cup thawed frozen reduced-fat nondairy whipped topping
1 container (6 ounces) low-fat custard-style apricot or peach-flavored yogurt
Mint sprigs (optional)

1. Preheat oven to 400°F. Cut phyllo dough crosswise into 4 pieces. Place 1 sheet phyllo dough on work surface. Keep remaining sheets covered with plastic wrap and damp kitchen towel. Lightly coat first sheet with cooking spray; place in large custard cup. Place second sheet on top of first, alternating corners; spray with cooking spray. Repeat with remaining 2 phyllo sheets, continuing to alternate corners. Repeat with remaining phyllo dough to form 6 strudel cups. Place custard cups on cookie sheet; bake about 15 minutes or until pastry is golden. Let cool to room temperature.

2. Meanwhile, combine blackberries and sugar in small bowl; let stand 15 minutes. Mix whipped topping and yogurt in medium bowl. Reserve ½ cup blackberries for garnish; gently stir remaining blackberries into whipped topping mixture. Spoon into cooled pastry cups. Garnish with mint. *Makes 6 servings*

Nutrients per Serving (1 strudel cup): Calories: 125, Total Fat: 4 g, Calories from Fat: 22%, Saturated Fat: <1 g, Cholesterol: 3 mg, Sodium: 22 mg, Carbohydrate: 25 g, Dietary Fiber: 3 g, Protein: 3 g

Dietary Exchanges: 1½ Fruit, 1 Fat

Butterscotch Bars

¾ **cup all-purpose flour**
½ **cup packed brown sugar**
½ **cup fat-free butterscotch ice cream topping**
¼ **cup cholesterol-free egg substitute**
3 **tablespoons butter or margarine, melted**
1 **teaspoon vanilla**
¼ **teaspoon salt**
½ **cup toasted chopped pecans (optional)**

1. Preheat oven to 350°F. Lightly coat 8-inch square baking pan with nonstick cooking spray; set aside.

2. Combine all ingredients in medium bowl; stir until blended. Spread into prepared pan.

3. Bake 15 to 18 minutes or until firm to touch. Cool completely in pan. Cut into 16 bars. *Makes 16 servings*

Tip: These sweet bars are the perfect packable treat. Wrap individually in plastic wrap so they will be ready to grab for the lunch box or a spur-of-the-moment picnic in the park.

Nutrients per Serving (1 bar): Calories: 103, Total Fat: 2 g, Calories from Fat: 21%, Saturated Fat: <1 g, Cholesterol: 6 mg, Sodium: 90 mg, Carbohydrate: 19 g, Dietary Fiber: <1 g, Protein: 1 g

Dietary Exchanges: 1 Starch, ½ Fat

Amy's Lemonade Mousse

1 quart cold fat-free (skim) milk
2 packages (1 ounce each) fat-free, sugar-free vanilla instant pudding mix
2 packages (½ ounce each) sugar-free powdered lemonade mix, undiluted
1 container (8 ounces) frozen fat-free nondairy whipped topping, thawed
Fresh or frozen mixed berries

1. Pour milk into large bowl. Add pudding mix and whisk 2 minutes until smooth. Whisk in powdered lemonade mix.

2. When mixture thickens, whisk in whipped topping until smooth. Pour into 8 parfait glasses. Chill. Garnish with berries. *Makes 8 servings*

Nutrients per Serving (about ½ cup): Calories: 120, Total Fat: <1 g, Calories from Fat: 9%, Saturated Fat: <1 g, Cholesterol: 2 mg, Sodium: 405 mg, Carbohydrate: 21 g, Dietary Fiber: 0 g, Protein: 4 g

Dietary Exchanges: 1 Starch, ½ Milk

Mangoes and
Sweet Cream

2 ounces reduced-fat cream cheese, softened
½ cup low-fat vanilla yogurt
1 packet sugar substitute
¼ teaspoon vanilla
1 ripe medium mango, peeled, seeded and diced *or* 1 cup diced peaches

1. Combine cream cheese, yogurt, sugar substitute and vanilla in small mixing bowl. Beat with electric mixer on medium speed until smooth. Fold in mangoes.

2. Spoon mixture into two dessert dishes.   *Makes 2 servings*

Nutrients per Serving (⅔ cup): Calories: 185, Total Fat: 5 g, Calories from Fat: 26%, Saturated Fat: 4 g, Cholesterol: 16 mg, Sodium: 175 mg, Carbohydrate: 28 g, Dietary Fiber: 2 g, Protein: 6 g

Dietary Exchanges: 2 Fruit, 1 Fat

Acknowledgments

The publisher would like to thank the companies and organizations listed below for the use of their recipes and photographs in this publication.

Chilean Fresh Fruit Association

Equal® sweetener

Heinz North America

Mott's® is a registered trademark of Mott's, LLP

Mrs. Dash®

National Cattlemen's Beef Association on Behalf of The Beef Checkoff

National Turkey Federation

Unilever

USA Rice Federation™

Wheat Foods Council

Wisconsin Milk Marketing Board

Index

Metric Conversion Chart

VOLUME MEASUREMENTS (dry)

$1/8$ teaspoon = 0.5 mL
$1/4$ teaspoon = 1 mL
$1/2$ teaspoon = 2 mL
$3/4$ teaspoon = 4 mL
1 teaspoon = 5 mL
1 tablespoon = 15 mL
2 tablespoons = 30 mL
$1/4$ cup = 60 mL
$1/3$ cup = 75 mL
$1/2$ cup = 125 mL
$2/3$ cup = 150 mL
$3/4$ cup = 175 mL
1 cup = 250 mL
2 cups = 1 pint = 500 mL
3 cups = 750 mL
4 cups = 1 quart = 1 L

VOLUME MEASUREMENTS (fluid)

1 fluid ounce (2 tablespoons) = 30 mL
4 fluid ounces ($1/2$ cup) = 125 mL
8 fluid ounces (1 cup) = 250 mL
12 fluid ounces ($1 1/2$ cups) = 375 mL
16 fluid ounces (2 cups) = 500 mL

WEIGHTS (mass)

$1/2$ ounce = 15 g
1 ounce = 30 g
3 ounces = 90 g
4 ounces = 120 g
8 ounces = 225 g
10 ounces = 285 g
12 ounces = 360 g
16 ounces = 1 pound = 450 g

DIMENSIONS

$1/16$ inch = 2 mm
$1/8$ inch = 3 mm
$1/4$ inch = 6 mm
$1/2$ inch = 1.5 cm
$3/4$ inch = 2 cm
1 inch = 2.5 cm

OVEN TEMPERATURES

250°F = 120°C
275°F = 140°C
300°F = 150°C
325°F = 160°C
350°F = 180°C
375°F = 190°C
400°F = 200°C
425°F = 220°C
450°F = 230°C

BAKING PAN SIZES

Utensil	Size in Inches/Quarts	Metric Volume	Size in Centimeters
Baking or Cake Pan (square or rectangular)	$8 \times 8 \times 2$	2 L	$20 \times 20 \times 5$
	$9 \times 9 \times 2$	2.5 L	$23 \times 23 \times 5$
	$12 \times 8 \times 2$	3 L	$30 \times 20 \times 5$
	$13 \times 9 \times 2$	3.5 L	$33 \times 23 \times 5$
Loaf Pan	$8 \times 4 \times 3$	1.5 L	$20 \times 10 \times 7$
	$9 \times 5 \times 3$	2 L	$23 \times 13 \times 7$
Round Layer Cake Pan	$8 \times 1 1/2$	1.2 L	20×4
	$9 \times 1 1/2$	1.5 L	23×4
Pie Plate	$8 \times 1 1/4$	750 mL	20×3
	$9 \times 1 1/4$	1 L	23×3
Baking Dish or Casserole	1 quart	1 L	—
	$1 1/2$ quart	1.5 L	—
	2 quart	2 L	—